The Nuts & Bolts of
SOUP TO NUTS
Cooking

by
Cindy & Jerry Herrell

ISBN: 978-1-62407-546-9

**Publication #14,213**
Printed in the United States of America.

To create your own custom cookbook, contact:
G&R Publishing
507 Industrial Street • Waverly, IA 50677
800-383-1679

books@gandrpublishing.com
www.gandrpublishing.com
www.facebook.com/gandrpublishing

Table of Contents

Appetizers, Beverages & Dips 1

Soups & Salads 11

Breads & Rolls 31

Vegetables & Side Dishes 39

Main Dishes & Meats 43

Desserts 55

Cookies & Candies 77

Miscellaneous 89

Kid's Kitchen Crafts

Cooking & Nutritional Tips

Household Hints

Index

Introducing SOUP TO NUTS

Cindy and I (Jerry) own a great Restaurant, with an Old Fashioned Soda Fountain, called Soup to Nuts, located in Northeastern Wisconsin. Our restaurant is known for delicious home cooked foods, great desserts and fabulous service, mainly because the food is prepared the same way at the restaurant as in our own home. Customers have been asking Cindy to write a cookbook for years to divulge her cooking secrets and recipes. Cindy has succumbed to their requests and has spent the last two years organizing her recipes that ranged from little scraps of paper, to those just hanging around in her brain, into a cookbook that is brimming with scrumptious soups & salads, main course delights and desserts that are great for all occasions. Most of the recipes are made with ingredients that are common in many homes; no specialty items or hard to find spices. After trying some of her recipes you will see why Soup to Nuts is one of the highest rated restaurants in the area. We hope you enjoy using "The Nuts and Bolts of SOUP TO NUTS Cooking".

Dedicated to the ones I love

I would like to dedicate this cookbook to the women who preceded me and taught me so much about cooking...and life. My Grandmother, Signora (a good Norwiegen girl), cooked professionally as a young woman in the early 1900's. In fact, it's how she met her husband...he loved her cooking too.

My Mom was also a good cook, probably learning a lot from her mother. Mom's real love was baking. though. She always made it look so effortless. Who knew you could whip together a pie crust so fast, or have chocolate chip cookies coming out of the kitchen at the drop of a hat? Whatever Mom made tasted great because of the love she put into it. And she's still at it!

Mom always let me "putter" in the kitchen, even at a fairly young age. Sometimes it was helping her with dinner, or teaching me how to make soups, pies and casseroles. As I got older, she let me experiment with new recipes and find my own way. Eventually I learned that cooking was natural for me as long as it was down home, taste good, not too complicated cooking. The busier we get these days, the better "simple" cooking sounds.

Over the years I've learned a lot from my Mother-in-law, my sisters-in-law and many friends. I also learned something important from my husband. Make it interesting, make it attractive, and make it fun! Jerry has, on occasion, offered to make dinner completely by himself. Did you know that brown meat and brown gravy with white potatoes are boring? How about adding a blue food coloring to the gravy? We still laugh about that solution. Green beans would have been my choice, but it wouldn't have been as much fun.

I hope you enjoy the recipes found in this book, and have an opportunity to make some memories of your own.

Angel By Your Side

May you always have an angel by your side watching out for you in all the things you do.
Reminding you to keep believing in brighter days,
Finding ways for wishes and dreams to take you to beautiful places.
Giving you hope that is as certain as the sun.
Giving you the strength of serenity as your guide.
May you always have love and comfort and courage,
And may you always have an angel by your side.

May you always have an angel by your side.
Someone there to catch you if you fall,
Encouraging your dreams,
Inspiring your happiness,
Holding your hand and helping you through it all.

In all our days, our lives are always changing.
Tears come along as well as smiles, along the roads you travel.
May the miles be a thousand times more lovely than lonely.
May they give you the kind of gifts that never, ever end,
Someone wonderful to love, and a dear friend in whom you can confide.
May you have rainbows after every storm,
May you have hopes to keep you warm,
And may you always have an angel by your side.

Emilia Larson

Appetizers, Beverages & Dips

CHIPPED BEEF DIP

1 1/3 C. mayonnaise
1 1/3 C. sour cream
2 tsp. dill weed
2 tsp. Beau Monde (from Spice Island)

2 T. dry minced onion
2 T. dry parsley
2 pkg. chipped beef

Mix all ingredients together thoroughly.
Refrigerate 2 hours or overnight to blend flavors. Serve with crackers.

BRAUNSCHWEIGER PARTY DIP

12 oz. Braunschweiger (liver sausage)
3 oz. cream cheese, softened
1/3 C. sour cream
1 tsp. lemon juice

1 tsp. onion, finely chopped or grated
Dash pepper
Dash garlic powder

Mix all ingredients together until smooth. Serve immediately. Optional: refrigerate for 1 hour then shape spread into ball and cover with cut up parsley. Serve with crackers.

BEER DIP

1/2 C. sour cream
16 oz. cream cheese
1 C. cheddar cheese, shredded
1 C. mayonnaise

1 pkg. Hidden Valley Ranch Dressing
1 or 2 green onions, chopped

Mix well and refrigerate until ready to serve. Serve with pretzels. It goes really well with your favorite beer. (and a football game)

ORIENTAL CHICKEN DIP

2 C. chicken, cooked and chopped
16 oz. onion & chive cream cheese
1/4 C. carrots, shredded
1 pkg. (4 oz.) almonds, slivered
1 tsp. ginger
1 tsp. garlic powder
2 tsp. soy sauce
Topping:
Sweet & sour sauce

Spread cream cheese on a platter. (reserve a little chicken and carrots to sprinkle on top) Mix the rest of ingredients and spread on top of the cream cheese. Sprinkle reserved chicken and carrots on top. Drizzle with Sweet & sour sauce just before serving. Serve with your favorite tortilla chips.

CHICKEN JALAPENO DIP

2 boneless, skinless chicken breasts
1 T. olive oil
8 oz. cream cheese, softened
1/4 C. mayonnaise
1/4 C. milk
1/4 C. red bell pepper, minced
2 T. jalapeno pepper, minced
1 T. lemon juice
3/4 tsp. salt
3/4 tsp. Tabasco sauce

Preheat oven to 375°. Heat oil in a 12" skillet over medium/high heat. Cook chicken, turning frequently, until tender and golden on all sides. Finely chop chicken. In a medium bowl combine all ingredients (including chicken) until well blended. Spoon mixture into a oven proof crock or small casserole dish. Bake at 375° for 20 minutes or until mixture is hot and bubbly. Serve with crisp crackers or pita triangles.

BEAN DIP

2-16 oz. can refried beans
1-16 oz. jar salsa
1 lb. Velveeta cheese

Empty beans and salsa into a 2 quart, microwave safe dish. Cut Velveeta into 1/2 x 1/2" cubes and stir into beans. Cover and microwave on high for 2 minutes. Stir until well blended. Cover and microwave another 2 minutes until heated through. Serve with taco chips.

TACO DIP

8 oz. ground beef
1-1/2 tsp. taco seasoning
1/2 C. water
1-16 oz. can refried beans
1/2 C. sour cream

1 C. shredded lettuce
1 C. tomatoes, chopped
1/2 C. onions, chopped
1/2 C. black olives, sliced
1 C. shredded cheddar, or Mexican blend cheese

Brown ground beef in skillet. Add taco seasoning and water and stir to blend. Bring to a boil and cook over medium heat for 15 minutes, or until water is cooked out and seasoning is well distributed. Cool. Using a 12" round platter (or similar size serving dish), spread beans across the bottom of dish, all the way to the edges. Spread the sour cream over the beans to about 1/2" from the edges. It will be thin. Sprinkle the prepared ground beef evenly on top. Layer the lettuce, tomatoes, onions, black olives and cheese on top, in that order. Cover and refrigerate until ready to serve. Serve with taco chips of your choice.

SALSA FRESCA (FRESH SALSA)

3-4 cloves of garlic, chopped fine
1 medium onion, chopped
2-3 fresh jalapenos, chopped fine
1/3 C. cilantro, finely chopped

4-6 large tomatoes, diced
1 T. Oil
Juice of one lime
1-2 green bell peppers, chopped

Mix all ingredients in medium bowl. Add salt and pepper if desired. Serve with tortilla chips.

The person who says it can not be done should not interrupt the person doing it.

FLORIDA CAVIAR

- 2 cans black eyed peas
- 1 can hominy
- 1 onion, chopped
- 1 C. green onion, chopped with stems and all
- 1 green pepper, chopped
- 2 medium tomatoes, diced
- 1 T. garlic, minced
- 1 T. parsley
- 1 small can green chilies, diced
- 2 C. Italian dressing

None of the above ingredients need to be drained. Combine all ingredients. Cover and refrigerate. Let marinate for 24 hours. Salt and pepper to taste. Use as dip with crackers or tortilla chips. (Fritos dippers work great)

TEXAS CAVIAR

- 1 can black eyed peas
- 1 can black beans
- 1 can pinto beans
- 1 can garbanzo beans
- 1 can white corn
- 1/2 C. red pepper, chopped
- 1/2 C. yellow pepper, chopped
- 1/2 C. green pepper, chopped
- 1/2 C. red onion, chopped
- 1/2 C. celery, chopped
- 3/8 tsp. salt
- 3/8 tsp. pepper
- 6 to 8 jalapeno, sliced and chopped

Dressing:
- 1 C. oil (canola)
- 1/3 C. sugar, heaping
- 1/3 pkg. Hidden Valley Ranch Dressing Mix
- 1/3 tsp. salt
- 2/3 C. apple cider vinegar

Rinse and drain all 5 cans and combine in a large mixing bowl. Add the peppers, onions, celery, salt, pepper, and jalapenos and mix well. In a sauce pan, combine oil, sugar, Hidden Valley Ranch Dressing, salt and vinegar. Heat on stove top until sugar dissolves. Cool. Blend dressing with the other mixture and serve as salsa or a dip with chips.

OLIVE CHEESE BALLS

8 oz. shredded cheddar cheese
1/2 C. flour
2 tsp. butter, room temperature
Dash cayenne (red pepper)
25 to 35 stuffed green olives

Mix cheese, flour, butter and pepper together in bowl. Wrap about 1 T. of mixture around each olive, completely covering it. Squeeze together in hand. The heat of your hand will make it hold together. Place each ball on ungreased cookie sheet about 2" apart. Bake at 400° for 15 minutes. Serve warm.

THREE IN ONE CHEESE BALL

8 oz. cream cheese, warm to room temperature
1 lb. shredded cheddar cheese
2 T. milk
2 T. onion, minced
2 T. Worchestershire sauce

1/2 C. bleu cheese, crumbled
1/4 tsp. garlic powder
Coarsely ground black pepper
Fresh parsley, minced
Pecans, finely chopped

In a mixing bowl combine cream cheese, shredded cheese, milk, onion and Worchestershire sauce. Beat till fluffy or process in food processor. Divide into thirds. Cover each portion with saran wrap and form into a ball. Unwrap one ball and roll in cracked pepper. Add bleu cheese to second ball and mix well. Reshape into a ball and roll in parsley. Add garlic to third portion and mix well. Reshape into a ball, roll in pecans. Cover each portion with saran wrap and refrigerate until ready to serve. Let stand at room temperature for 1 hour before serving. Serve with crackers

The most positive way to progress to the top is to start at the bottom and never stop.

SHRIMP BALL

1-8 oz. pkg. cream cheese, softened
4 1/2 oz. can shrimp, drained
1 1/2 tsp. onion, minced

1 tsp. seasoning salt
1/2 tsp. lemon juice
1 C. pecans, chopped

Mix the cream cheese, shrimp, onion, seasoning salt and lemon juice until well blended. Form into a ball. (To form ball, scrape mixture onto a piece of saran wrap. Pull up saran around mixture and form ball from the outside of wrap.) Unwrap the ball and roll in chopped pecans. Serve with crackers.

SALMON BALL

8 oz. cream cheese, warm to room temperature
1/2 C. small curd cottage cheese
1/4 C. onion, finely chopped
1 tsp. herb vegetable seasoning

1/2 tsp. thyme leaves
1 garlic clove, minced
1-15 1/2 oz can salmon, drained and flaked
3/4 C. parsley, chopped

Combine cream cheese, cottage cheese, onion, seasonings and garlic in a mixing bowl and blend well. Stir in salmon until well blended. Wrap in Saran Wrap and chill 3 hours or overnight. Shape into ball while still in Saran Wrap. Unwrap and roll in parsley. Serve with crackers.

Lying in bed would be an altogether perfect experience, if one had colored pencils long enough to draw on the ceiling.

SALMON MOUSSE

13 oz. water packed Salmon, drained and cleaned
8 oz. cream cheese, softened
1 C. Miracle Whip
1/2 C. celery, finely chopped
1/2 C. shallots, chives, or green peppers, chopped
1 envelope Knox gelatin
1/3 cup cold water
1 can (10 3/4 oz) tomato soup

In a medium bowl, mix salmon, cream cheese, miracle whip, celery and shallots together. In a separate bowl, mix gelatin with 1/3 cup cold water and let sit for about 10 minutes. Put soup in a sauce pan (no water) and bring to a boil. Cool slightly. Add gelatin and salmon mixture to soup and mix thoroughly with a beater or whisk. Put into a greased mold, cover with plastic wrap and refrigerate for 3 to 4 hours (overnight is best). To serve, invert mold onto serving plate. Tap on bottom of mold so it releases. Serve with crackers.

CHEESY CRAB ROLL UPS

20 slices white bread
1/2 lb. Velveeta cheese, cubed
1 lb. butter, divided
1 to 2 cans Crabmeat, drained & flaked

Trim crust from bread. Flatten bread with rolling pin. Melt Velveeta and 1/2 Lb butter in a sauce pan over low heat. Cool, then stir in crab meat. Spread the mixture onto the bread slices and roll up. Melt remaining butter. Brush bread rolls with butter. Place seam side down on cookie sheet or 9" x 13" cake pan. Cover and freeze. When ready to use, remove from freezer. Cut rolls into three or four pieces. Place on ungreased cookie sheet. Bake at 400° for 15 minutes or until lightly browned. Yield 60 to 80 roll ups.

CAPPUCCINO MIX

1 C. instant coffee creamer
1 C. instant chocolate drink mix
2/3 C. instant coffee crystals
1/2 cup sugar
1/2 tsp. ground cinnamon
1/4 tsp. ground nutmeg

Combine all ingredients and mix well. Store mix in an airtight container. To prepare one serving, add 3 T. of the mix to 6 oz. of hot water. Stir well.

PRALINE COFFEE

3 C. brewed coffee
3/4 C. Half & Half (or cream)
3/4 C. brown sugar
2 T. butter
3/4 C. maple syrup

Heat the coffee, cream, brown sugar and butter in saucepan, but don't boil. Add the maple syrup. Pour into coffee cups and garnish with whipped cream. Makes 4-6 servings.

SPICED TEA

1 C. instant iced tea mix
2 C. sugar
2 small pkg. dry lemonade mix (like Kool Aid)
1-14 oz. jar Tang
2 tsp. cinnamon
2 tsp. ground cloves

Blend all ingredients thoroughly in a large bowl. Store in an air tight container (like a quart canning jar). Use 2-3 T. of mix for each cup of hot or iced tea.

FROSTY ORANGE JUICE

1 C. orange juice
1/2 tsp. vanilla
1/4 C. sugar
1/2 C. milk
4-5 ice cubes

Place all ingredients in blender. Pulse until the ice cubes are reduced to small pieces and juice is frothy. Makes 1 serving.

BANANA BERRY SHAKE

1 C. frozen unsweetened strawberries
1 small banana, sliced
1/4 C. milk
1 C. vanilla ice cream

Place berries, banana and milk in blender. Process until smooth. Add ice cream and continue blending until incorporated. For a lower calorie version, replace the ice cream with low fat yogurt, use skim milk, and add 3-4 ice cubes. Makes 1 serving.

BRANDY SLUSH

2 C. boiling water
4 green tea bags
7 C. water
2 C. sugar
12 oz. frozen orange juice concentrate

12 oz. frozen lemonade concentrate
2 C. Brandy (or Vodka)

Let tea bags steep in 2 cups of boiling water about 20 minutes. Squeeze out bags and discard. Boil 7 cups of water with sugar to make a syrup. Cool. Combine the tea mixture with the syrup. Add orange juice, lemonade and Brandy. Place in a freezable container and freeze until ready to use. Make at least 24 hours in advance. To serve, fill glass 1/2 full with slush. Top with Sprite, 7 Up, or sour soda. Stir. Garnish with fruit.

BAILEY'S IRISH CREAM

1-14 oz. can Eagle Brand sweetened condensed milk
12 oz. whipping cream (not whipped)
3 eggs

1 C. Brandy or Whiskey
1 1/2 T. chocolate syrup
1/4 tsp. coconut or almond extract

Blend all ingredients in blender for about 30 seconds or until well blended. Store in jar in refrigerator. Shake well before serving. It will keep in refrigerator for several weeks. Enjoy!

CHERRY BOUNCE (LIQUOR)

1 1/2 qt. fresh tart cherries (or raspberries, or blackberries)
1 1/2 C. water

1 1/2 C. sugar
1 qt. Vodka

Wash cherries (no need to pit them) and place in a glass gallon jar (with lid). Add all other ingredients and shake well. Since the cherries are usually ready to pick in mid July, this would be the time to make cherry bounce. It does not need to be refrigerated. Shake every other day until Christmas time. If desired, re-bottle the liquid and discard the cherries. Makes a nice sipping liquor.

NOTES

Soups & Salads

BEEF BARLEY SOUP

1 lb. sirloin or round steak
1/2-1 C. flour
3-4 T. Canola oil
20 C. water
4 T. beef base (or 4 bullion cubes)
3 bay leaves
2 cloves of garlic, minced
1 onion, chopped
2 C. celery, chopped
1 green pepper, chopped
3 medium potatoes, peeled and cubed
1 C. barley
1/2 tsp. each, salt and pepper

Cut the steak into bite sized pieces. Put flour into a gallon size zip lock bag. Add the beef pieces, close the bag, and shake the bag until beef is coated with flour. In a large soup kettle, heat the oil. When the oil is hot, add the beef and brown on all sides. Turn the heat to low setting and gradually add water, beef base, bay leaves, garlic, onions, celery, and green pepper. Simmer about 30 minutes. Add potatoes, barley, salt, and pepper. Continue cooking another 20-30 minutes or until potatoes are done.

STUFFED GREEN PEPPER SOUP

2 C. cooked white rice
2 lbs. ground beef
2 C. onions, chopped
2 C. celery, chopped
2 cloves garlic, minced
2-28 oz. cans tomato sauce
2-28 oz. cans diced tomatoes
4 C. green pepper, diced into 1" squares
1 tsp. black pepper
2 tsp salt
1/4 C. brown sugar
2 tsp. beef base, or 2 bouillon cubes

Cook rice according to package directions. Set aside. In large soup pot, brown ground beef, onions and celery. Drain excess fat. Add remaining ingredients, except rice. Bring to a boil, reduce heat and simmer for 30-40 minutes or until vegetables are tender. Add rice and serve.

BEEF TORTELLINI SOUP

12 C. water
6 tsp. beef base (or 6 bouillon cubes)
24 oz. tomato juice
1 medium onion, chopped
2 C. celery, sliced
16 oz. pkg. frozen mixed vegetables
6 C. beef filled tortellini noodles
Salt and pepper

Combine water, beef base and tomato juice in a large soup pot. Bring to a boil. Add onions and celery, then reduce heat and simmer for 20-30 minutes. Add frozen vegetables and tortellini noodles. Simmer for another 20-30 minutes. Salt and pepper to taste.

SPAGHETTI SOUP

2 lbs. Hamburger
1 large onion, chopped
2 C. celery, chopped
1-2 C. green peppers, chopped
20 C. water
3 T. beef base
3 cans (15 oz) diced tomatoes
1 T. oregano
1 T. basil
1 T. Minced garlic
16 oz fresh mushrooms, sliced
8 oz spaghetti noodles, broken into 2" pieces

Brown hamburger, onions, celery, and green peppers in a soup pot. Drain excess grease. Add water, beef base, tomatoes, & seasonings. Simmer 20-30 minutes. Add the mushrooms and spaghetti noodles (broken into 2" lengths). Simmer 15-20 minutes more. Makes a large kettle of soup. (This recipe can be cut in half.) Garlic toast is an excellent side to serve with this.

CHICKEN NOODLE SOUP

12 C. water
6 tsp. chicken base
3 whole bay leaves
1 C. onion, diced
1 C. celery, diced
3 C. diced cooked chicken
3 C. frozen mixed vegetables
2 C. egg noodles
Salt & pepper to taste

Bring the water and chicken base to a boil. Add onions, celery, bay leaves, and chicken. Simmer for 30 minutes. Add frozen vegetables and continue cooking for 15 more minutes. The noodles can be added 10 minutes before serving. Salt and pepper to taste.

CREAM OF ASPARAGUS SOUP

1 stick butter or margarine
1 large onion, chopped
1 C. celery, sliced
1 C. flour
2 C. chicken broth
2 C. milk
1-12 oz. can evaporated milk
3 C. fresh asparagus, cleaned, cut in 1" pieces
Salt and pepper to taste

Melt butter in soup pot. Add onion and celery, cook until vegetables are tender. Blend flour into onion mixture to make a paste. Gradually add chicken broth, milk and evaporated milk. Cook over medium heat until soup begins to thicken, stirring constantly. (Cream soups burn very easily.) Clean and cut asparagus. Place in a microwave safe bowl with 1/2 cup water. Cover and microwave for 2 minutes. Stir and continue cooking for another 2 minutes. Add asparagus and cooking water to soup. Season soup with salt and pepper and cook until asparagus is tender and soup is thickened. If soup becomes too thick, add a little milk or water.

CORN & SAUSAGE CHOWDER

1/2 C. butter or margarine
1 medium onion, chopped
1 C. celery, sliced
1 C. carrots, sliced in medallions
1/2 C. flour
1 T. Parsley
1 tsp. dried thyme (or 1 T. Fresh thyme)
6 C. chicken broth
2 bay leaves
2 C. milk
2 medium potatoes, unpeeled and diced
1 C. frozen corn
1-10 oz. pkg. frozen creamed corn
2 C. shredded cabbage
1/2 lb. sausage (like kielbasa or polish sausage)
2 T. Cider vinegar
1 tsp. salt
1/8 tsp. ground red pepper

Melt butter in soup pot. Add onion, celery, and carrots and sauté until vegetables are tender. Stir in parsley, thyme and flour to make a paste. Gradually add chicken broth and bay leaves. Cook and stir until it starts to thicken. Dice potatoes. Place potatoes in a microwave safe dish with 1/2 cup water. Cook for 3 minutes. Slice the sausage, then quarter each slice to make small pieces. Add milk, potatoes, corn, cabbage and sausage. Cook 15-20 minutes or until cabbage is tender. Stir in vinegar, salt and pepper. Thin with a little water or milk if necessary.

WISCONSIN BEER CHEESE SOUP

1 stick butter or margarine
1/2 C. diced carrots
1/2 C. diced celery
1/2 C. chopped onion
1 clove of garlic, minced
1 C. Flour
1/2 tsp. salt

1/2 tsp. paprika
Dash of pepper
2 C. chicken broth
2 C. milk
2 C. flat beer
3 C. (12 oz.) shredded cheddar cheese

Melt butter in soup pot. Add vegetables and garlic and cook until tender. Stir in flour and seasonings to make a paste. Slowly add chicken broth. Stir until soup begins to thicken. Gradually add milk and beer, stirring constantly until thickened. Add cheese. Simmer until heated through. If soup becomes too thick, add more milk to thin. Top each serving with bacon bits or seasoned croutons, if desired.

CLAM CHOWDER

1/2 Lb. butter or margarine
1 large onion, sliced & quartered
2 C. flour
4 C. chicken broth
4 C. 2% milk

3 cans minced clams
2 cans (12 oz) evaporated milk
4 C. cubed potatoes
1/2 tsp. Salt
1 tsp. pepper

Melt butter in soup kettle. Add onions and sauté lightly until onions are translucent. Blend flour into the onion mixture. Slowly add chicken broth, stirring as you go. Gradually add evaporated milk, stirring constantly. Open the clams and empty the entire content of the cans (including the clam juice) into the kettle along with milk. Cook over low heat, stirring constantly, until soup starts to thicken. Add potatoes and cook for another 20-30 minutes. (Cubed potatoes can be pre-cooked in the microwave, if desired.) Salt and pepper to taste. Simmer till thick and the potatoes are done, add more milk as necessary.

POTATO SOUP

10 C. diced potatoes
1-2 onions, chopped
1 stick butter or margarine
1 can of evaporated milk
2 C. milk
12 oz. Velveeta cheese
2 T. flour
Salt and pepper

Place potatoes in soup pot. Cover with water and bring to a boil. Reduce heat and simmer about 15-20 minutes or until potatoes are tender. Do not drain. While potatoes are cooking, sauté the onions in the butter. Add the onions, evaporated milk and 1 1/2 cups of milk to the potatoes. Stir well. Cube the cheese so it melts easier, then add to the soup. Put remaining 1/2 cup of milk in a small bowl with a tightly covered lid. Add 2 T of flour and shake until blended. Stir this into the soup along with salt and pepper. Continue stirring until soup is thick and heated through. Each serving can be garnished with bacon bits, parsley, or chives.

SPLIT PEA SOUP

1 lb. dry split peas
1 large onion, chopped
2 C. celery, chopped
3 bay leaves
1 ham bone, or 2 C. diced leftover ham
2 C. carrots, sliced into thin medallions
4 red potatoes, peeled and diced
1 tsp. salt
1 tsp. pepper

Rinse peas in colander. Place peas in soup pot with 8 cups of water. Add onion, celery, bay leaves and ham bone. Bring to a boil. Reduce heat, cover and simmer for 1-1 1/2 hours. Add carrots and potatoes. Continue cooking for about an hour or until vegetables are tender and peas are smooth. Remove ham bone. Take off any ham still on the bone and return the meat to the soup. Add salt and pepper. If soup gets too thick, add a little water.

CREAM OF BROCCOLI SOUP

2 sticks of margarine or butter
1 large onion, chopped
2 C. flour
4 C. chicken broth
4 C. milk
2-12 oz. cans evaporated milk
2-16 oz. pkgs. frozen broccoli (or 4 C. raw)
2 C. shredded cheddar cheese (optional)
Salt and pepper to taste

In large soup pot, melt butter. Add onions and cook until onions are translucent. Stir in flour to make a roux. Gradually add the chicken broth, then the milk and evaporated milk. Cook over medium heat, stirring constantly until soup begins to thicken. Cut the broccoli into bite sized pieces. Wash and add to the soup. Continue cooking for an additional 20-30 minutes or until vegetables are tender. If soup thickens too much, add more milk a little at a time. If desired, stir in cheese 10 minutes before serving. Season with salt and pepper to taste.

TOMATO BASIL SOUP

2 large cans tomato juice
1 T. onion powder
2 T. dried sweet basil
1 tsp. salt
Dash of pepper
2 tsp. sugar
4 C. milk
1/2 C. flour

Open tomato juice and pour into a soup kettle. Add onion powder, basil, salt, pepper, and sugar. Bring to a boil over medium heat, stirring regularly. Put one cup of the milk into a small bowl with a tight fitting lid. Add the flour to the milk, secure the lid , and shake vigorously for one minute. Check to make sure all lumps are gone, then add to the soup. Add the remainder of the milk, stirring constantly, until soup is thickened and heated through.

VEGETABLE CHEESE SOUP

2 medium potatoes, peeled and diced
1/2 C. onion, chopped
1/2 C. celery, chopped
1/2 C. carrot, chopped
3 C. water
1 T. chicken base
1 1/2 C. frozen mixed vegetables
1 can cream of chicken soup, undiluted
1/2 lb. Velveeta cheese, cubed

Combine potatoes, onion, celery, carrots, water, and chicken base in soup pot. Bring to a boil, reduce heat, then cover and simmer for 10-15 minutes, or until potatoes are tender. Add mixed vegetables and cream of chicken soup. Return to boil. Simmer for another 10 minutes. Stir in cheese just until melted. Do not let it boil.

TACO SOUP

1 lb. lean hamburger
1 onion, chopped
2 C. celery, chopped
1 green pepper, chopped
1 can (16 oz.) chili beans
1 can (16 oz.) pinto beans
1 can (16 oz.) corn
1 can (16 oz.) diced tomatoes
1 can (16 oz.) stewed, Mexican tomatoes
1 can (16 oz.) tomatoes with chilies
1 small can green chilies
1 pkg. taco seasoning mix (dry)
1 pkg. ranch dressing mix (dry)
1 can sliced black olives (optional)
1/2 C. shredded cheddar cheese (optional)
1 tsp. cumin
1/2 tsp. each, salt and pepper

In a large soup pot, brown beef, onion, celery, and green pepper. Drain excess fat. Add all other ingredients except olives and cheese. Stir until thoroughly mixed. Bring to a boil, lower heat, and simmer for one hour. Garnish each bowl with olives and shredded cheese, if desired.

CALIFORNIA MEDLY

2 sticks margarine or butter
1 onion, chopped
2 C. celery, chopped
2 C. flour
4 C. chicken broth
4 C. milk

2-12 oz. can evaporated milk
1-16 oz. pkg. frozen broccoli (or 2 C. raw)
1-16 oz. pkg. frozen cauliflower (or 2 C. raw)
2 C. carrots, cut into medallions
Salt and pepper to taste

Melt the margarine in soup pot. Add onions and celery. Cook until the vegetables are tender. Stir in the flour and make a paste. Gradually add the chicken broth, milk, and evaporated milk, stirring constantly. Cook the broccoli, covered, in the microwave with 1/3 cup water for 3 minutes. Add to the soup. Cook the cauliflower and the carrots in the same way (separately). These vegetables can be added directly to the soup, but it will take a lot longer and there is more of a chance of burning the soup. Cook and stir until thickened, the vegetables are tender, and the soup is heated through. If soup becomes too thick, add more milk, a little at a time. Add salt and pepper if needed.

BEAN SOUP

1 lb. navy beans or pinto beans
1 onion, chopped
1 C. celery, chopped
2 C. carrots, cut in thin medallions
1 ham bone, or 2 C. leftover ham, cut in 1/2" pieces

1 tsp. salt
1 tsp. pepper
1 tsp. cumin
3 bay leaves

Sort and rinse beans. This is important because there can be rocks and dirt in the beans. Place beans in large soup pot with 6-8 cups of water. Bring to a boil for 5 minutes. Turn off heat and let stand for 1 hour. Drain beans into a colander and rinse. Clean out soup pot. Add beans, ham bone and 8 cups of clean water. Bring to a boil, then turn down heat to simmer for 1 hour, stirring occasionally. Add remaining ingredients and cook for another 1 1/2 to 2 hours, or until beans and vegetables are tender. Soup should have a thick and creamy look. Remove ham bone and let cool slightly. Pick the remaining meat off the bone and return the meat to the soup. Individual servings may be topped with chopped onions and shredded cheese.

CALICO BEAN SOUP

2 lbs. pinto beans, dry
2 lbs. navy beans, dry
1 lb. butter beans, dry
2 lbs. kidney beans, dry
1 lb. split peas, dry
1 lb. lentils, dry
1 lb. black beans, dry
1 large onion, chopped
4 stalks celery, chopped
1 green pepper, chopped
5 carrots, washed and sliced
1 ham bone, or 2 C. diced salt pork, or 2 C. diced ham
3 bay leaves
1 tsp. cumin
1 tsp. salt
1 tsp. pepper
1 T. minced garlic
1-16 oz. can diced tomatoes
Sour cream
Shredded cheddar cheese

Mix all dry beans together. Take out 4 cups for soup and store the remainder in an air tight container for future use. Rinse the 4 cups of mixed beans and put in soup pot. Cover with water (1" above beans). Bring to a boil and cook for 5 minutes. Remove from heat and let stand for 1 hour. Rinse beans in colander. Return to pot and add water to cover beans. Add onions, celery, green peppers, carrots and ham bone. Bring to a boil, reduce heat and simmer 2-3 hours or until beans are tender. Add more water if necessary. Add bay leaves, cumin, salt, pepper, garlic and tomatoes. Cook another 5-10 minutes. Top each serving with sour cream and shredded cheese, if desired.

WHITE CHILI

1 lb. chicken, cooked and diced (4 breasts)
48 oz. great northern beans
16 oz. medium salsa
16 oz. mild salsa
1 tsp. cumin
1-4 oz. can green chilies
8-12 oz. shredded Monterey jack cheese

Cook chicken and dice. Add all the other ingredients. Mix well and cook until thoroughly heated. Serve with corn bread. If desired, sprinkle each serving with additional shredded cheese.

CHICKEN PASTA SALAD

4 chicken breasts, cooked and cubed
12 oz. elbow macaroni
2 C. sliced celery
2 C. red or black grapes, cut in half
1/2 red onion, chopped
1 C. chopped walnuts (optional)
1 C. mayonnaise
1 C. Miracle whip

Cook and cube chicken breasts, or use canned chicken to save time. Prepare macaroni according to package directions. Drain and rinse in cold water. Place all ingredients in large bowl. Thoroughly mix together. Refrigerate at least one hour before serving. Makes 6 - 10 servings.

SEAFOOD NOODLE SALAD

1 pkg. fine egg noodles
1 can crab or 1 C. imitation crab, broken in pieces
2 cans shrimp or 8 oz. salad shrimp, broken
1 T. Pimento, chopped
2 green onions, chopped
Mayonnaise
1 T. Vinegar
Salt and pepper

Boil noodles according to package directions. Drain and cool. Add remaining ingredients and enough mayonnaise to moisten. Add vinegar and salt and pepper to taste. Refrigerate for about an hour to let flavors blend before serving. This salad looks nice served on a lettuce leaf with fruit and a croissant on the side.

Life is a mystery to be lived, not a problem to be solved.

TORTELLINI CAESAR SALAD

9 oz. frozen cheese tortellini
8 C. torn romaine lettuce
1/3 C. shredded parmesan cheese
1 C. seasoned croutons
1 C. cherry tomatoes, cut in half (optional)

DRESSING:
1/2 C. mayonnaise
1/4 C. milk
1/4 C. shredded parmesan cheese
2 T. Lemon juice
2 garlic cloves, minced

Cook tortellini according to package directions. Drain and rinse in cold water. Place in a large salad bowl. Add the romaine and 1/3 cup parmesan cheese. In a small bowl, combine all dressing ingredients. Mix well. Just before serving, drizzle with dressing and toss to coat. Top with croutons and tomatoes.

BLT PASTA SALAD

2 C. cooked elbow macaroni (4 oz. uncooked)
2 C. tomatoes, chopped
4-6 slices bacon, cooked and crumbled
1-1/2 C. iceberg lettuce, thinly sliced

1/4 C. mayonnaise
1/4 C. sour cream
2 tsp. Dijon mustard
1/2 tsp. sugar
1 tsp. cider vinegar
1/4 tsp. salt
1/4 tsp. pepper

Combine macaroni, tomatoes, bacon and lettuce in a large bowl. Toss gently. In separate bowl, mix mayonnaise, sour cream, mustard, sugar, vinegar, salt and pepper. Stir well. Add dressing to salad mixture. Toss gently. Serve immediately. Serves 4-5.

CRAB PASTA SALAD

1 lb. Imitation crab
12 oz. pkg. of small shell pasta
1/2 medium red onion, chopped
1 can (15 oz.) sliced black olives
1 C. celery, sliced
1 C. (approximately) Ranch dressing

Cook pasta according to package directions. Do not over cook. Drain and rinse in cold water. Place pasta in large bowl. Break crab apart so it looks shredded, add to pasta. Thinly slice red onion, then cut each slice into about eight pieces. Drain black olives. Add onions, black olives, celery, and dressing to bowl. Thoroughly mix all together. Add more ranch dressing if necessary. Refrigerate at least one hour before serving. It may be necessary to add more dressing before serving, as it may be absorbed during refrigeration. Makes 4 servings.

CHINESE SALAD

1/2 C. butter or margarine
2 pkgs. Ramon noodles, crushed (discard seasoning)
3-4 oz. slivered almonds
1/2 C. sunflower seeds
1 head Napa cabbage
5 green onions, sliced, including greens

DRESSING:
1 C. sugar
1/2 C. red wine vinegar
2 T. Soy sauce
1 C. Canola oil

Sauté butter, Ramon noodles, almonds and sunflower seeds until toasted and lightly browned. Set aside. Cut the Napa cabbage in half. Then thinly slice diagonally. Add green onions and toss to mix. Set aside and make dressing. Mix sugar, vinegar, soy sauce and oil together in a small covered bowl. Occasionally shake to keep mixed. Just before serving, mix all parts together. This salad can be made ahead and put together at the last minute.

TACO SALAD

2 C. torn lettuce
4 oz. already prepared taco meat
1/3 C. chopped tomatoes
1/4 C. chopped red onions
1/4 C. sliced black olives

1/4 C. banana peppers
1/4 C. shredded mozzarella or Mexican cheese
Salsa
Sour Cream
Taco chips or baked tortilla bowl (optional)

Baked tortilla bowls are not hard to make. You will need an appropriate size oven proof pan or bowl and 10" flour tortilla shells. Place the bowl up side down and drape the tortilla over the bowl. Bake in 325° oven for 8 minutes. Taco meat is prepared according to package directions, using 1 lb. of ground beef and 1 package of taco seasoning mix. Divide into 4 equal servings. Put salad together by layering the first seven ingredients in order. The salad can be made in the tortilla bowl or on a dinner plate. Serve the salsa and sour cream on the side, as a dressing. If serving on a plate, the tortilla chips can be added to the edge. This recipe is for an individual serving.
NOTE: Additional ingredients can be added or substituted, such as black beans, avocados, peppers or jicama.

CHICKEN TACO SALAD

1 C. onion, chopped
2 C. chicken, cooked and diced
1-16 oz. can pinto beans, rinsed and drained
1/2 C. water
1 pkg. taco seasoning mix
6 C. shredded lettuce

2 C. tomatoes, chopped
1/2 C. green pepper, chopped
1 C. shredded cheddar cheese
2 C. Corn Chex
Salsa
Sour cream

Sauté onion in large pan sprayed with non stick cooking spray. Stir in chicken, pinto beans, water and taco seasoning. Mix well to combine. Bring to a boil, then lower heat and simmer for 1 minutes, stirring occasionally. Meanwhile, in a large serving bowl, combine lettuce, tomato and green pepper. Spoon hot chicken mixture over lettuce mixture. Top with cheese and Corn Chex. Toss gently.
Note: For individual servings, divide lettuce mixture among 6 plates. Divide chicken into 6 portions and place on top of lettuce. Top with cheese and Corn Chex. Makes 6 servings.

SESAME CHICKEN SALAD

4-4 oz. chicken breasts
8-10 C. mixed lettuce greens
1 C. corn
1/2 C. green onions, sliced
4 radishes, sliced
1 small can mandarin oranges
4 tsp. sesame seeds, toasted

Dressing:
1/2 C. orange juice
1/4 C. rice vinegar, or white vinegar
1/2 tsp. toasted sesame oil, or canola oil
1/4 tsp. pepper

Cook chicken in small amount of oil until no longer pink in center. Cube chicken, divide into 4 servings, and set aside. On 4 dinner plates, layer lettuce, chicken, corn, onions, radishes and oranges. In a separate container with lid, combine orange juice, vinegar, oil, and pepper. Cover and shake well. Divide dressing among 4 salads. Pour over salads or serve on the side. Sprinkle sesame seeds over top. (To toast seeds, cook and stir in non stick skillet for 1-2 minutes, until golden brown.)

CRAB SALAD

2 C. torn lettuce
4 oz. imitation crab, shredded
1/4 C. red onion
1/4 C. mandarin oranges
1/4 C. sliced black olives
1/8 C. sliced almonds
1/4 C. Chinese noodles

This recipe is for an individual serving. Arrange lettuce on a dinner plate. Spread shredded crab on top. Thinly slice red onion, then quarter the slices. Sprinkle on salad. Continue layering oranges, olives, almonds and noodles. Serve with dressing on the side. This salad is great with Honey Mustard, but also with French or Ranch dressing.

GRILLED CHICKEN SALAD

2 C. torn lettuce
1 grilled chicken breast
1/3 C. sliced celery
1/3 C. chopped tomatoes
1/4 C. lightly chopped walnuts

Season chicken breast with Lawry's seasoning salt and black pepper. Grill in lightly oiled pan until no longer pink in the middle. Meanwhile, layer lettuce, celery, tomatoes and walnuts on a dinner plate. When chicken is done, slice in 5-6 slices and put on top of prepared plate. Serve dressing on the side. This recipe is for an individual serving.

RAW VEGGIE SALAD

SUGGESTED VEGETABLES:
Cauliflower
Broccoli
Red onion
Jicama
Carrots
Celery
Cucumbers
Red or green peppers
Grape tomatoes
DRESSING:
2 C. Miracle Whip
1 C. sour cream
1/4 C. sugar
1 tsp. garlic salt
1 tsp onion salt

Start with a combination of raw vegetables, cut up
into bite sized pieces. Plan for approximately one cup of each, but you can use more of one and less of another (like onions) if you choose. Mix them all together into a large bowl. Mix Miracle Whip, sour cream, sugar, garlic salt and onion salt together. Stir into cut up, mixed vegetables and mix thoroughly. Let the salad sit in the refrigerator for at least an hour before serving.

JICAMA SALAD

1 Bunch broccoli flowerets
1/2 lb. bacon, fried and crumbled
1 C. raisins
1/2 C. dry roasted peanuts
1/2 C. red onion, chopped
1 medium jicama, peeled and cubed
DRESSING:
1 C. mayonnaise
3 T. vinegar
1/4 C. sugar

Place broccoli, bacon, raisins, peanuts, onions and jicama in a large bowl. Broccoli should be cut into bite sized pieces. Whisk together mayonnaise, vinegar and sugar in a small bowl. Pour over salad ingredients and gently mix until everything is evenly coated. Marinate overnight. Serve chilled as a side dish or as a main course lunch.

NUTTY CHICKEN SALAD

3 C. cubed, cooked chicken
1/2 C. walnuts, coarsely chopped
1 C. celery, sliced crosswise
1 C. mayonnaise (not Miracle Whip)

Cook chicken and chop in small pieces. Cool, Mix all ingredients together in a large bowl making sure everything is well coated with the mayonnaise. Refrigerate for one hour before serving. Serve in a tomato cup on lettuce or as a sandwich on toasted bread with lettuce and tomato slices. Serves 6-8.

SEVEN LAYER SALAD

6 C. head lettuce, torn into bite sized pieces
1/2 red onion, thinly sliced, cut in half
1 C. celery, chopped
2-3 C. frozen peas, thawed
6-8 slices bacon, cooked crisp and crumbled
2-3 C. mayonnaise
1 C. cheddar cheese, shredded

In a glass 9" x 13" pan, layer ingredients in order, starting with the lettuce. Spread the mayonnaise layer thinly across the top. Sprinkle the shredded cheese on top of mayonnaise. Cover and refrigerate for at least one hour before serving. Makes 6-8 servings.

TUNA SALAD

Large Batch
66 oz. canned tuna
1 1/3 C. Celery, finely chopped
2/3 C. Onion, finely chopped
1/3 C. Lemon juice
1 1/3 C. Pickle relish
1 3/4 -2 C. Mayonnaise (not Miracle Whip)

Small Batch
4 oz. Canned tuna
2 T. Celery, finely chopped
1 T. Onion, finely chopped
1/2 T. Lemon juice
2 T. Pickle relish
3 T. Mayonnaise (not Miracle Whip)

Open and thoroughly drain tuna. Break up tuna into small pieces with hands. Mix all ingredients together except mayo. Add mayo and mix thoroughly. This recipe for mixing up your tuna can be used for tuna sandwiches, tuna melts and tuna salad. Note: For a nice looking salad, start with a bed of lettuce on a dinner plate. Cut a medium sized tomato into eight wedges, but don't cut all the way through the bottom of the tomato. Place the tomato in the center of the lettuce and open like a flower. Put a scoop of tuna mixture into the tomato. Garnish the salad with veggies like carrots, cucumbers and radishes. Small batch is 1 serving

CLASSIC WALDORF SALAD

1/2 C. raisins
2 1/2 C. apples, chopped into bite sized pieces
1/2 C. sliced celery
1/2 C. walnut pieces

2/3 C. mayonnaise
1 T. Lemon juice
Pinch of salt
2-4 C. torn lettuce

Choose a crisp, red apple, such as Gala, Braeburn, or Macintosh. Mix together raisins, apples, celery, walnuts, mayo, lemon juice and salt in a large bowl. Serve on a bed of lettuce.

VARIATION WALDORF SALAD

1/2 C. raisins
2 1/2 C. apples, chopped into bite sized pieces
1/2 C. sliced celery

1/2 C. walnut pieces
4 C. torn lettuce, leaf and head combined

Combine all ingredients in large salad bowl. Toss gently to mix. Serve with dressing on the side. Ranch, Honey Mustard or Raspberry Vinegarette all go well with this salad.

STRAWBERRY SPINACH SALAD

1/4 C. sliced almonds, toasted
1 1/2 C. fresh strawberries, cleaned and sliced
1/2 medium cucumber, sliced and cut in half
1/2 small red onion, sliced into thin rings
6-8 oz. fresh spinach

DRESSING:
1 lemon (or 4 T. bottled lemon juice)
4 T. white wine vinegar
2/3 C. sugar
2 T. Canola oil
2 tsp. poppy seeds

Preheat oven to 350°. Spread almonds in single layer in a 9" square pan. Bake 10-12 minutes or until lightly toasted. Cool and set aside. Zest lemon, measuring 1 tsp. of lemon zest. Juice lemon, measuring 4 T. of juice. Combine lemon zest, lemon juice, vinegar, sugar, oil and poppy seeds in a small bowl. Whisk until well blended. Cover and refrigerate until ready to use. Just before serving, place the spinach, strawberries, cucumber, and onion in a salad bowl. Pour dressing over salad and gently toss to coat. Sprinkle with almonds.
NOTE: If strawberries are not in season, try substituting chopped apples (1 1/2 cups) and craisins (1/2 Cup).

KITCHEN SINK SALAD

4 C. torn leaf lettuce
4 C. torn head lettuce
1-2 C. finely chopped red cabbage
1/2 red onion, sliced in thin rings, separated
1 C. carrots, cut in coins
1 C. celery, sliced crosswise
1/2 green pepper, cut in bite sized pieces
1/2 red pepper, cut in bite sized pieces

1/2 C. banana peppers, sliced
1/2 C. dill pickles, chopped
1 C. sliced black olives (optional)
1 C. sliced mushrooms
2 C. cubed ham
1-2 C. cubed cheese (cheddar or mozzarella)
2 medium tomatoes, chopped
2-3 hard boiled eggs
1/4 C. sunflower seeds
1-2 C. croutons

Place all ingredients, except eggs, sunflower seeds, and croutons in a very large bowl. Toss until well mixed. Just before serving, top with 2-3 hard boiled eggs, cooled and sliced, sunflower seeds, and croutons. Serve with your choice of dressing. To make a smaller salad, cut all ingredients in half. Add or delete items as desired.

SIMPLE LEMON DRESSING

1 C. lemon juice
2 C. Canola oil

1 tsp. black pepper

Put all ingredients into a covered container and shake well. This dressing will settle, so shake before each use. Great as a low calorie dressing. Add other herbs, spices, garlic, or Dijon mustard to change the taste.

1000 ISLAND DRESSING

1 C. Miracle whip
1 C. tomato ketchup

1/3 C. pickle relish

Combine all ingredients in a small bowl. Whisk until well blended. Cover and refrigerate any leftover dressing.

BUTTERMILK FRUIT SALAD

1 qt. Buttermilk
3 small (3 oz.) pkgs. French Vanilla Instant Pudding
8 oz. Cool Whip
32 oz. Fruit Cocktail, drained
32 oz. canned pineapple chunks, drained
3 small cans mandarin oranges, drained
3 C. grapes, purple or green, cut in half
2 bananas, sliced, if desired

Whisk the buttermilk and pudding mix together for about one minute. Gently fold in the Cool Whip. Make sure the cans of fruit are drained well. Add fruit to the pudding mixture and stir gently. If not serving right away, omit the bananas and add them at the last minute. Recipe is generous, serves a crowd. NOTE: To make a lower calorie version of this salad, use skim milk, sugar free pudding and light Cool Whip.

POTATO SALAD

10-12 medium sized red potatoes
8 hard boiled eggs
1 medium yellow onion, chopped
2 C. celery, chopped
8-10 radishes, sliced
1 medium cucumber, peeled and sliced (optional)
1 C. mayonnaise
1 C. miracle whip
3 T. yellow mustard, or 1 T. dry mustard

Wash potatoes. Put in large kettle and cover with water. Add 1 tsp salt and bring to a boil. Boil for about 20 minutes or until tender when poked with a fork. Drain and cool. (Potatoes and eggs can be made ahead and kept in the refrigerator till ready to put the salad together.) When potatoes are cool, you may peel if you choose or leave the skins on. Cut potatoes into bite size pieces. Chop 6 of the eggs, using an egg slicer and cutting in two direction. Save two of the eggs for the top. In a large bowl, mix potatoes, eggs, onions celery, radishes, and cucumbers. Add the mayonnaise, Miracle Whip, mustard, and salt and pepper to taste. Gently mix all ingredients together. Place potato salad in large serving bowl and arrange sliced hard boiled eggs on top. If desired, sprinkle top lightly with paprika. Cover and refrigerate for two hours or overnight.

Breads & Rolls

BUTTERMILK BREAD (BREAD MAKER RECIPE)

3/4 C. water
1/2 C. buttermilk
1 tsp. lemon juice
2 T. canola oil

3 C. bread flour
1 tsp. salt
2 T. dark brown sugar
2 1/4 tsp. active dry yeast

Following instructions for bread maker, place water, buttermilk, lemon juice and oil in bread pan. Layer flour, salt and brown sugar. Add yeast last. Start bread maker. If possible, open lid during first mix cycle to check consistency of dough. Add more bread flour if dough is too moist. Add water (1 tsp. at a time) if dough is too dry. Close lid and let bread maker run through its cycle. This is a very generous sized loaf.

OATMEAL BREAD (BREAD MAKER RECIPE)

1 1/8 to 1 1/4 C. water
1/4 C. honey or molasses
1 T. butter or margarine, softened
2 C. bread flour

1/2 C. quick cooking oats
1 tsp. salt
1 1/4 tsp. dry active yeast

Following instructions for bread maker, put water, honey and butter in bread maker. Top with flour, oats. Salt and yeast. Start bread maker. Pillsbury bread flour works best for me. Using honey will result in a lighter colored bread, molasses will be darker. This recipe can be used with the timed delay setting.

BEER BREAD (THE EASIEST BREAD RECIPE EVER)

3 C. self rising flour
3 T. sugar
12 oz. beer

1/4 C. melted margarine or butter

Mix flour and sugar together. Add beer and mix well. Put into a lightly sprayed bread pan. Pour melted butter over top. Bake at 350° for 30 minutes. Serve warm.
Note: Add 1 cup shredded Cheddar Cheese to the mix as an option.

PIZZA DOUGH

1 pkg. active dry yeast　　3 C. flour
1 tsp. sugar　　　　　　　 1/2 tsp. salt
1 C. warm water　　　　　 2 T. Canola oil

Dissolve the yeast and sugar in warm water. Using a fork, beat in half of the flour. Add salt, oil, and remaining flour. Mix well. Knead on a lightly floured surface until smooth, adding more flour, if needed. Put a little oil on hands and cover dough with oil. Place dough in lightly oiled bowl. Cover and let rise in a warm place until doubled in size. Divide dough in half. On lightly floured surface, roll each half into a 13" circle. Place dough on pizza pan, which has been lightly oiled. Brush top of dough lightly with oil. Spread with sauce, cheese, meat, mushrooms, etc. Bake at 450° for 10-25 minutes.

FLOUR TORTILLAS

2 C. flour　　　　　　　　1/4 C. shortening
1 tsp. salt　　　　　　　　 1/2 C. warm water
1/2 tsp. baking powder

Mix flour, salt and baking powder. Cut in shortening with pastry blender. Gradually add water to make a stiff dough. Knead on lightly floured surface until dough is "springy". Divide into 12 balls. Cover and allow to rest for 20-30 minutes. On lightly floured surface, roll each ball into an 8" circle. Heat a heavy frying pan over medium heat. Place each tortilla on ungreased fry pan (one at a time). Cook until tortilla is speckled brown, about 1 1/2-2 minutes. Turn over and cook the other side the same. If tortilla puffs up while cooking, just press it down. Place finished tortillas in tortilla warmer to serve.

PEANUT BUTTER BREAD

2 C. flour　　　　　　　　Pinch salt
1/2 C. sugar　　　　　　　1/2 C. peanut butter
4 tsp. baking powder　　　 1 1/2 C. milk

Mix the flour, sugar, baking powder and salt together. Add the milk and peanut butter. Mix well. Put the mixture into a 5" x 9" bread pan that is sprayed with cooking spray. Bake at 350° for 40 to 50 minutes or until done. Let rest for 5 to 10 minutes. Remove from pan and let cool.

PECAN PUMPKIN BREAD

1 C. oil
2/3 C. water
4 eggs
3 C. sugar
16 oz. can cooked mashed
  pumpkin
2 1/2 C. white flour

1 C. whole wheat flour
2 tsp. baking soda
2 tsp. cinnamon
1 1/2 tsp. salt
1 tsp. nutmeg
1 C. pecans, chopped

Grease two 5" x 9" loaf pans (or 5 mini loaf pans). Mix oil, water, eggs, and sugar together. Add pumpkin and stir until blended. Sift flour, wheat flour, soda, cinnamon, salt and nutmeg into separate bowl. Add to pumpkin mixture and mix well. Fold in pecans. Pour batter evenly into prepared pans. Bake 60 to 70 minutes at 350°. Cool 10 minutes. Remove from pans.

LEMONY ZUCCHINI BREAD

4 eggs
1 1/4 C. milk
1 C. canola oil
3 T. lemon extract
4 C. flour
1 1/2 C. sugar
1 pkg. instant lemon pudding

1 1/2 tsp. baking soda
1 tsp. baking powder
1 tsp. salt
2 C. zucchini, shredded
1/4 C. poppy seeds
2 tsp. lemon zest

Whisk eggs, milk, oil and lemon extract in a bowl. In another bowl, sift flour, sugar, pudding, baking soda, baking powder and salt. Stir the dry ingredients into liquid mixture until just moistened. Fold in Zucchini, poppy seeds and lemon zest. Pour into 2 greased 5" x 9" pans and bake at 350° for 50 to 55 minutes. Cool 10 minutes before removing from pans.

CHOCOLATE ZUCCHINI BREAD

3 eggs, beaten
1 C. canola oil
2 C. sugar
1 T. vanilla
2 C. zucchini, peeled and shredded
2 1/2 C. flour

1/2 C. baking cocoa
1 tsp. salt
1 tsp. cinnamon
1/4 tsp. baking powder
1 tsp. baking soda
1 C. mini chocolate chips
1/2 C. walnuts, chopped

Mix eggs, oil, sugar and vanilla together. Add zucchini. In a separate bowl, sift flour, cocoa, salt, cinnamon, baking powder and baking soda together. Add dry ingredients to zucchini mixture and mix well. Fold chips and nuts into mixture. Pour into 2 lightly sprayed 5" x 9" loaf pans. Bake at 350° for 1 hour or until done. Let cool 10 minutes. Remove from pans.

LEMON POPPYSEED BREAD

1 C. hot water
1 stick butter or margarine, softened
4 eggs, beaten
1 pkg. Lemon cake mix

1 pkg. instant lemon pudding mix
1/4 C. poppy seed
Topping:
Juice of 1 lemon
1/4 C. powdered sugar

Place water and butter in mixer bowl, gently mix together. Add eggs, and beat well. Gradually add cake mix and pudding mix. Beat on medium/high for 1 to 2 minutes. Fold in poppy seeds. Lightly spray 2 (5" x 9") bread loaf pans. Divide mixture into prepared pans. Bake at 350° for 45 minutes or until done. Let cool 10 minutes and remove from pans. Meanwhile, mix powdered sugar with lemon juice to make a glaze. Drizzle over bread while hot.

ZUCCHINI BREAD / MUFFINS

3 eggs, beaten
2 C. sugar
1 C. oil
3 tsp. vanilla
3 C. flour
1 tsp. salt

1 tsp. baking soda
3 tsp. cinnamon
2 C. zucchini, grated
Optional:
1 C. walnuts, chopped
1 C. chocolate chips or raisins

Mix eggs, sugar, oil and vanilla together. Sift flour, salt, baking soda and cinnamon in a separate bowl. Add dry ingredients to egg mixture alternately with zucchini. Fold in walnuts and chips. Spray two 5" x 9" loaf pans (or use 5 mini loaf pans). Divide batter evenly between prepared pans. Bake as follows: Two 5" x 9" loaves, bake at 350° for 1 hour. Five mini loaves, bake at 350° for 45 to 50 minutes. Muffins, bake 350° for 20 minutes.

EVER READY BRAN MUFFINS
(OUR FAMILY'S TRADITIONAL EASTER BREAKFAST)

15 oz. box raisin bran cereal
3 C. sugar
5 C. flour
5 tsp. baking soda
1 T. + 1 tsp. pumpkin pie spice

2 tsp. salt
4 eggs, beaten
1 C. butter or margarine, melted
1 qt. buttermilk

In large bowl, mix raisin bran cereal, sugar, flour, baking soda, pumpkin pie spice and salt. Add eggs and buttermilk and mix well. Stir in melted margarine until thoroughly mixed. Store in a covered container in refrigerator and use as desired. For muffins fill sprayed pan 2/3 full. Bake at 400° for 20 minutes. Batter will keep in refrigerator for up to 6 weeks.

OATMEAL APPLE RAISIN MUFFINS

1 egg, beaten
3/4 C. milk
1 C. raisin
1 C. apples, finely chopped
1/2 C. canola oil
1 C. flour

1 C. quick oats
1/3 C. sugar
3 tsp. baking soda
1 tsp. salt
1 tsp. cinnamon
1 tsp. nutmeg

Mix egg, milk, raisins, apple and oil. In a separate bowl, sift together flour, sugar, baking soda, salt, cinnamon and nutmeg. Add oatmeal and sifted dry ingredients alternately to egg mixture, and mix until just moistened. Pour batter into paper lined or sprayed muffin pans. Bake at 400° for 15 to 20 minutes.

OATMEAL PANCAKES

1 C. quick oatmeal
1 C. hot water
1 C. milk
1/8 C. sugar
1 tsp. salt

2 eggs, beaten
3 tsp. canola oil
1/2 tsp. baking soda
1/2 tsp. baking powder
1 1/4 C. flour

Boil water. Put oatmeal in a bowl, then add hot water. Let stand a few minutes so oatmeal cooks. Add milk, sugar, eggs and oil. Mix well. In a separate bowl, sift flour, baking soda and baking powder together. Add to oatmeal mixture and mix until well blended. Let rest for 5 minutes. Preheat griddle to med/high heat. Spray with non stick spray. Drop batter onto hot griddle. When first side is lightly browned, flip pancake and brown on second side (2-3 minutes on each side). Serve with applesauce or maple syrup. Serves 2.

GINGERBREAD PANCAKES

1 C. unbleached flour
2 tsp. baking powder
1 tsp. cocoa
1/2 tsp. ginger, powdered
1/4 tsp. cinnamon, ground

1/4 tsp. cloves, ground
2 T. hazelnuts, ground
1 C. skim milk
2 egg whites
2 T. dark molasses

Sift flour, baking powder, cocoa, ginger, cinnamon and cloves into large bowl. Set aside. In another bowl, beat milk, egg whites and molasses together. Add the hazelnuts. Add the hazelnut mixture to the dry ingredients. Do not over mix, lumps are okay. Coat a non stick pan with spray. Preheat pan to med/high heat. (Be sure to wait until pan is preheated.) Use 2 T. batter per pancake. Cook for 2 minutes then flip and cook for 2 more minutes or till done. Serves 4

*Peace of mind is not the absence of conflict from life,
but the ability to cope with it.*

NOTES

Vegetables & Side Dishes

MOM'S HOME MADE EGG NOODLES

3 eggs
1 tsp. nutmeg
2-2 1/2 C. flour

Beat the eggs and nutmeg well. Gradually add flour until it becomes of dough consistency. It should be a little less dry than pie crust. Roll out on a lightly floured surface to 1/8" thickness. Let dry for about 1 hour. Turn dough over, cut into sections (about 5" x 5") and let dry again for about an hour. Cut into thin strips with a butter knife. Drop into boiling soup or boiling water. Cook for approximately 10-12 minutes or until tender. Noodles can be made ahead and kept in a baggie in the refrigerator for a day or two.

GERMAN SPAETZLE

4 C. flour
4 eggs, beaten
1 tsp. salt
2 C. milk

Place flour and salt in a large bowl. Make a well in the center. Stir in the eggs and milk until well blended. Let stand 10-15 minutes. Meanwhile, bring a pot of water (6-8 cups) to a boil. Press the dough through a Spaetzle maker or a metal colander into the boiling water. Cook until the noodles float. Drain. Rinse in cool water. Drain again. Turn out onto paper towel to blot up some of the water. To serve, fry gently in melted butter.

CREAMED CORN CASSEROLE

1 can whole kernel corn
1 can creamed corn
1 small box corn bread muffin mix
8 oz. sour cream
1 stick butter, melted
1 egg, beaten
1-4 oz. can green chilies (optional)

In large bowl, mix all ingredients together. Butter or spray a 9" x 9" pan (or use a 7" x 11"pan). Pour mixture into prepared pan. Bake at 400° for about 45 minutes. Serve warm.

OVEN BAKED POTATO WEDGES

1/2 C. Canola oil
4 Large Potatoes
1 medium onion, diced

Ground pepper
Lawry's seasoning salt

Wash potatoes and cut lengthwise into 8 wedges. Place oil, onion and potatoes into a gallon baggie. Roll bag around to coat potatoes with oil and onion. Dump contents of baggie onto a 11" x 17" jelly roll pan (roasting pan also works). Sprinkle the potatoes with the seasoning and pepper. Preheat oven to 425°, bake for 30 minutes, turning occasionally, till brown (you can add a little more seasoning after turning potatoes if you like more spice). Serve with sour cream or ranch dressing.

SCALLOPED POTATOES

1 can soup: either cream of mushroom, cream of celery, cheddar cheese or cream of chicken (undiluted)
1/2 C. milk

1/2 tsp. pepper
4 C. potatoes, thinly sliced
1 small onion, thinly sliced
1 T. butter or margarine
1/4 tsp. paprika

In a small bowl, combine the soup, milk and pepper. Butter or spray a 1-1/2 quart casserole dish. Arrange alternate layers of potatoes, onion and sauce(at least 2-3 layers of each). Dot the top with butter. Sprinkle with paprika. Cover and bake at 375° for 1 1/4 hours. Uncover and bake 15 minutes more. Makes about 4 cups.

The early bird still has to eat worms.

SLICED BAKED POTATOES

4 medium potatoes (of similar size)
3 T. melted butter
1 tsp. salt
3 T. fresh or dried herbs, chopped (like parsley, chives, thyme, or sage)
1 tsp. seasoning salt (Lawry's)
4 T. Cheddar cheese, grated
1 1/2 T. Parmesan cheese

Wash potatoes and pat dry. Cut into thin slices, but don't cut all the way through. Slices should remain attached at the bottom of the potato. Place potatoes in a microwave safe dish. Drizzle with butter. Sprinkle with seasoning and herbs. Microwave at full power for 8-10 minutes, changing the position of the potatoes after 5 minutes. Let rest for 5 minutes. Sprinkle with cheeses and microwave for another 4-6 minutes at full power. Cheese should be melted and potatoes soft. Salt to taste.

HASH BROWN CASSEROLE

8 slices of bacon, cooked, drained and crumbled
1 small onion, diced
2 lb. bag of frozen, shredded hash browns
2 cans cream of mushroom soup
8 oz. sour cream
1/2 C. mayonnaise
1 can water chestnuts
8 oz. shredded cheddar cheese
1 tsp. salt
1/2 tsp. pepper

Cook bacon till crisp. Set on paper towel to drain. Sauté onion in bacon grease. Drain. Combine all ingredients in a large bowl and mix well. Lightly spray a 9" x 13" pan. Pour potato mixture into prepared pan. Bake at 400° for 40 minutes.

CALICO BEANS

1 lb. hamburger
1/2 lb. bacon, diced
1 large onion, chopped
1/2 C. ketchup
2 tsp. salt
4 tsp. vinegar
1/2 C. brown sugar
2 tsp. yellow mustard

30 oz. Pork & Beans, do not strain
15 oz. Butter Beans, strain
10 oz. Lima Beans, strain
15 oz. Kidney Beans, rinse with water, drain
15 oz. Black Beans, rinse with water, drain
15 oz. Pinto Beans, strain

This is a great dish to take to picnics or family reunions. Therefore, I usually make it in a small Nesco roaster, so it's portable. Brown the hamburger, bacon and onion in a frying pan or right in the roaster. Drain excess grease. Put all the cans of beans into the roaster. Note that some of the beans need to drained or rinsed. Add the ketchup, salt, vinegar, brown sugar and mustard and mix well. Simmer at 325° for about 45 minutes, stirring occasionally.

VEGETABLE PIZZA

2 pkg. crescent rolls
1 pkg. Hidden Valley Ranch Dressing Mix
1/2 to 3/4 C. Mayonnaise
8 oz. cream cheese
Any and all fresh vegetables of your liking; 1 C. each, washed and chopped
Broccoli

Cauliflower
Carrots
Radishes
Onions
Peppers
Tomatoes
OPTIONAL:
Shredded cheese and olives

Spread rolls out in a jelly roll pan, covering entire pan, being sure to go up the sides. Seal seams. Bake rolls for 8-10 minutes at 375°. Cool. Combine cream cheese, mayonnaise and dressing and blend together in bowl. Once crescent crust has cooled, spread cream cheese mixture over it. Finely chop fresh vegetables and spread over cheese layer, pressing gently into cream cheese. Sprinkle cheese and olives on top, if desired. Cover and refrigerate until ready to serve.

Main Dishes & Meats

PEAS 'N' RICE HOT DISH

1 lb. of lean ground beef
1 med. onion, chopped
2-3 stalks celery, chopped
1 med. green pepper, chopped
1/2 tsp. salt
1/2 tsp. pepper
2 cans tomato soup
1 can peas
1 C. uncooked minute rice

Place onions, celery and green pepper in (4 quart) kettle. Crumble ground beef into kettle. Cover and cook over medium heat until beef is browned and vegetables are tender. Drain. Add salt, pepper, tomato soup and peas. Heat thoroughly. Add a little water if necessary (maybe 1/2 cup). When it becomes hot and bubbly, add rice. Lower the heat to simmer, cover and cook 5 minutes longer. Serves four. Mom always served this dish with home made bread and butter.

SPAGETTI AND MEATBALLS

1 lb. ground beef
1 small onion, chopped
2 stalks celery, chopped
1 T. minced garlic
2 eggs
1/2 tsp. salt
1/2 tsp. pepper
1 C. finely crushed soda crackers
1-26 oz. jar spaghetti sauce
(if you like more sauce, add another jar of sauce)
8 oz. spaghetti noodles, dry

Crumble hamburger into a large bowl. Add onion, celery, garlic, eggs, salt, pepper and cracker crumbs. Mix well with hands. Shape into meatballs, 2" in diameter. Gently place in deep kettle and brown on all sides, turning frequently. When no longer pink in center, drain grease. Add spaghetti sauce. Cover and simmer for 10-15 minutes. Meanwhile, cook noodles according to package directions. Drain. Add 2 T. oil to noodles and toss to prevent from sticking together. Serve noodles and spaghetti in separate bowls, with garlic bread on the side.

LASAGNA

2 lb. ground beef
2 tsp. minced garlic
1 T. basil
1 1/2 tsp. salt
2 - 26 oz. jars spaghetti sauce
12 lasagna noodles
3 C. cottage cheese

1/2 C. Parmesan cheese
2 T. parsley flakes
2 beaten eggs
2 tsp. Salt
1/2 tsp. pepper
1 lb. shredded mozzarella cheese (divided in half)

Brown beef and drain fat. Add garlic, basil, salt and spaghetti sauce and simmer for 30 minutes. In separate large pot, cook lasagna noodles according to package directions. Drain, rinse, and set aside. In a separate bowl mix the cottage cheese, Parmesan cheese, parsley, eggs, salt and pepper together. Set aside. Place 1/2 the noodles in a 10" X 15" lasagna pan. Spread with 1/2 the cottage cheese mixture. Add half of the shredded cheese and half of the meat sauce. Repeat another layer of the same. Bake at 325° for 25 to 30 Minutes. Let stand for 10 minutes before cutting.
NOTE: This can be made ahead and refrigerated. If refrigerated, allow 15 minutes more in oven.

MEATLOAF

2 lbs. ground beef
2 eggs
1 envelope onion soup mix
1 T. minced garlic
1 tsp. salt
1 tsp. pepper
2/3 C. ketchup

1/4 C. water
1 C. seasoned bread crumbs
GLAZE:
1/2 C. ketchup
2 T. brown sugar
1 T. Worcestershire

Combine beef, eggs, soup mix, garlic, salt, pepper, 2/3 cup ketchup, water and bread crumbs in large bowl. Mix with your hands. Place into 5" X 9" loaf pan. Press firmly down to get the air out and leave the top flat. Bake at 350° for 40 minutes. In a small bowl, mix 1/2 cup ketchup, brown sugar and Worcestershire sauce. After meatloaf has baked for 40 minutes, spread Glaze on top and bake for an additional 15 minutes.

PIZZA HOT DISH

1 1/2 lb. hamburger
1 onion, chopped
1 tsp. garlic, minced
1 T. oregano
1/2 tsp. pepper
1/2 tsp. salt

1-15 1/2 oz. jar spaghetti sauce
8 oz. can tomato sauce
1/2 bag dumpling noodles
1 can cheddar cheese soup
1/2 to 1 lb. mozzarella cheese

Brown beef and drain fat. Add onion, garlic, oregano, salt and pepper and cook until onions are soft. Add spaghetti sauce and tomato sauce, simmer for 30 minutes. Cook noodles according to package directions. Add cooked dumpling noodles and 1 can cheddar cheese soup. Mix well. Pour into 9" X 13" pan or casserole dish. Sprinkle with 1/2 to 1 lb. shredded cheese to cover top. Cover and bake at 350° for 1 hour.
NOTE: Can be made in a small Nesco roaster for pot luck suppers.

DEEP DISH PIZZA

1 lb. ground beef
1-15 oz. can chunky tomato sauce
1-10 oz. can refrigerated pizza crust dough
6 oz. shredded mozzarella cheese

1 C. mushrooms, cleaned and sliced
1/2 C. onions, chopped
1/2 C. green peppers, chopped
1/2 C. black olives, sliced

Crumble beef in skillet and cook until browned. Drain. Add tomato sauce and cook until heated through. While meat is cooking, spray a 9" x 13" pan with non stick cooking spray. Unroll pizza dough and press evenly into bottom and sides of pan. Sprinkle half the cheese on crust. Top with meat mixture. Add vegetables. Bake uncovered at 425° for 12 minutes. Sprinkle remaining cheese on top of pizza and bake an additional 5 minutes or until crust is brown and cheese is melted. Cool a few minutes before cutting and serving.

BEEF TIPS

2 1/2 lb. beef sirloin, cubed
2 1/2 T. oil
2 1/2 C. beef broth
1/2 C. cranberry juice, or red wine
2 1/2 T. soy sauce
2 tsp. garlic, minced
1/2 tsp. onion salt
4 T. cornstarch
1 C. water

Brown meat in oil. Add broth, juice, soy sauce, garlic and onion salt. Simmer for 1 hour. In a separate container add cornstarch to cool water, cover and shake well. Add to beef mixture and stir till it thickens. Serve over mashed potatoes, rice or noodles.

BEEF STROGANOFF

1/3 C. butter, or canola oil
1 C. onion, chopped
1 tsp. garlic salt
2 cans mushrooms, sliced (or 8 oz. fresh mushrooms)
2 lb. beef sirloin or round steak
3 T. flour
2 C. beef broth
1 C. sour cream
2 tsp. Worcestershire sauce

Melt 2 T. butter in large skillet. Add garlic salt, onion, and mushrooms. Cook till soft. Set aside. Cut meat into 1/2" x 1" strips and brown with remaining butter, salt and pepper. Remove meat from pan and add flour to remaining butter in skillet, stirring to make a paste. Add beef broth, sour cream, onion mixture, Worcestershire sauce and meat. Simmer for about 1/2 hour. Serve over hot egg noodles.

A person is a success when others are better off for having associated with them.

JERRY BURGER

2 lb. lean ground chuck beef
1 tsp. Lawry's seasoning
1/2 tsp. salt
1/2 tsp. pepper

2 eggs
2 oz. saltine crackers, crushed
   (not pulverized)

Mix all ingredients together in a large bowl. Form the mixture into 8 ounce balls. Flatten into patties approximately 6" in diameter. To make a great burger cook the patty to 155° internal temperature. Add a slice of your favorite cheese and allow it to melt. Cut, butter, and grill the bun while cooking the burger. Add lettuce, tomato, onion and pickles for a delicious burger.
Note: The Jerry Burger is the "Cadillac" of burgers served at Soup to Nuts in Crivitz, WI.

CHOP SUEY

2 1/2 lb. beef, cubed
1/2 C. water or beef broth
1 Lg. can Chinese vegetables,
   drain but save liquid
1 Lg. can (or 2 small), bean
   sprouts with liquid

1 can water chestnuts, sliced
3 T. Worcestershire sauce
2 T. soy sauce
3 to 4 T. cornstarch

Spray a 10" skillet with non stick spray. Over medium high heat, brown beef. Add water, lower heat, cover and simmer for 30 minutes. Add vegetables, bean sprouts, water chestnuts, Worcestershire sauce and soy sauce. Simmer another 10 minutes. In a separate container with lid, add cornstarch to saved liquid. Cover and shake to blend. Add to meat mixture stirring till thickened. Serve over rice.

SPICY BROCCOLI BEEF STIR FRY

8 oz. pkg. fine spaghetti noodles
1/2 C. orange juice
1 T. cornstarch
2 T. soy sauce
2 tsp. sugar
1/8 tsp. cayenne pepper
1/4 tsp. crushed red pepper flakes

1 lb. beef sirloin, sliced thin
1 medium onion, sliced, separated into rings
1 clove garlic
3 C. fresh broccoli florets
1 small red bell pepper, cut into thin strips

Cook spaghetti to desired doneness as directed on package. Drain and cover to keep warm. Meanwhile, in a small bowl, combine orange juice, cornstarch, soy sauce, sugar and peppers. Cover and shake until well blended. Set aside. Spray a large non stick skillet or wok with non stick spray. Heat to medium/high heat. Add beef, onion and garlic. Cook and stir 3-5 minutes or until beef is no longer pink. Add broccoli and bell pepper, cover, and cook 2-4 more minutes, or until vegetables are crisp tender, stirring occasionally. Add sauce and cook until thickened and bubbly. Serve over warm spaghetti.

CHICKEN STIR FRY

2 T. oil
2-4 oz. chicken breasts
1/2 tsp. Lawry's Seasoning Salt
1 C. broccoli, chopped
1 C. cauliflower, chopped
1/2 C. celery, chopped
1/2 C. onion, chopped
1 C. zucchini, cut into 1/2 x 1/2 x 1" pieces

1 can water chestnuts
1-2 C. carrots, sliced
1 C. peppers, sliced (red or green)
1 tsp. minced garlic
2 T. soy sauce
1/8 tsp. cayenne pepper, optional

Coat bottom of a large skillet or wok with oil. Turn to medium/high heat. When hot, add chicken, season with Lawry's and cook until juices run clear. Remove from pan and cut into bite sized pieces. Meanwhile, add veggies of your choice (any or all of the above). Add garlic. Add more oil if necessary. Cook and stir until vegetables are crisp tender. Return chicken to vegetable mixture. Season with more Lawry's if desired and add cayenne pepper. Stir in soy sauce to coat. Cook 1-2 minutes more. Serve over rice.

MEXICAN LASAGNA

- 1 lb. lean ground beef
- 1/2 C. celery, chopped
- 1/2 C. onion, chopped
- 1 T. minced garlic
- 1/4 C. green pepper, chopped
- 1-14 oz. can tomatoes, crushed
- 1-14 oz. can enchilada sauce
- 1 tsp. salt
- 1/2 tsp. pepper
- 4 slices American cheese
- 1 C. low fat cottage cheese
- 1 egg, beaten
- 6 medium flour tortillas, cut into 3 strips

Brown beef with celery, onion, garlic and pepper. Drain fat. Add tomatoes, enchilada sauce, salt and pepper. Bring to a boil, reduce heat, and simmer for 10 minutes. Meanwhile, combine cheese, cottage cheese and egg in food processor. Pulse until cheese is broken up. Spread 1/3 of the meat mixture into a 9" x 13" pan. Spoon 1/2 the cheese mixture on meat. Top with 1/2 the tortillas. Repeat layers, ending with meat. Bake at 350° for 25 minutes. Let stand for 5 minutes before cutting. Serves 6.

SPICY TORTILLA BAKE

- 1 lb. lean ground beef
- 1-15 oz. can dark red kidney beans
- 1-28 oz. can diced tomatoes
- 1-4 oz. can green chilies
- 1 pkg. taco seasoning
- 6-10" flour tortillas, or 12-6" corn tortillas
- 1 C. shredded cheddar cheese

In large skillet, brown ground beef. Drain. Add beans, tomatoes, chilies and taco seasoning and heat thoroughly. Reduce heat and simmer for 5 minutes. Spray a 9" x 13" pan with non stick cooking spray. Cut tortillas in half. Layer half in bottom of pan, spread half of meat mixture on tortillas. Repeat layers. Top with cheese. Cover and bake at 350° for 25 minutes.

CHICKEN ENCHILADAS

4 Chicken Breasts (1 1/4 Lb) cooked and diced
2 C. chicken broth
1 can cream of chicken soup
1 small can diced green chilies
1 onion, finely chopped
10 to 12 -10" flour tortillas
1 lb. shredded Monterrey Jack cheese
12 oz. sour cream

Cook the chicken, broth, chicken soup, chilies and onions into a well blended sauce. Put a little sauce in the bottom of a 9" X 13" cake pan. Heat tortilla shells so they are pliable (microwave 2 to 3 shells for 30 seconds). Fill each shell with about 1/3 cup chicken sauce, 1 oz. Monterrey Jack and 1 oz. sour cream. Roll up shells place in pan seam down. Pour remaining chicken sauce on top. Sprinkle with remaining cheese. Bake at 350° for about 30 Minutes or until hot.

THREE CHEESE ENCHILADAS

1 1/2 C. (6 oz) shredded Monterrey Jack cheese, divided
1 1/2 C. (6 oz) shredded cheddar cheese, divided
3 oz. cream cheese
1 C. Pace picante sauce, divided
1 medium red bell pepper, diced
1/2 C. sliced green onion
1 tsp. cumin
8 flour tortillas (7" to 8")
2 C. shredded lettuce
1 C. chopped tomatoes

Combine 1 cup of Monterrey Jack, 1 cup Cheddar Cheese, cream cheese, 1/4 cup picante sauce, red pepper, onion & cumin. Mix well. Spoon 1/4 cup cheese mixture down center of each tortilla. Roll and place seam side down in 9" X 13" baking dish. Spoon remaining picante sauce evenly over enchiladas then cover with remaining cheese mixture. Bake at 350° for about 20 Minutes or until hot. Top with lettuce and tomatoes. Serve with additional picante sauce. Makes 4 Servings.

MEXICAN CASSEROLE

10-6" flour tortillas, halved
3 C. chicken, cooked and cubed
1 C. frozen corn
1 onion, chopped
1/2 green pepper, chopped
1-14 oz. can stewed tomatoes
1-10 oz. can diced tomatoes with green chilies
1 C. shredded mozzarella cheese

Spray a 9" x 13" pan with non stick cooking spray. Line with half the tortillas. Layer with chicken, corn, onion, pepper and stewed tomatoes. Cover with remaining tortillas. Pour tomatoes with green chilies over top. Cover and bake at 350° for 30 minutes or until heated through. Uncover and sprinkle with cheese. Bake uncovered for 10 more minutes or until cheese is melted. Serve with sour cream and salsa.

CHICKEN DIVAN

2 pkg. frozen broccoli, cooked lightly
4 chicken breast, cooked and cut in pieces
1 can cream of chicken soup
1/2 C. mayonnaise
1 tsp. lemon juice
1 C. shredded cheddar cheese
1 C. bread crumbs
2 T. margarine, melted

Lightly spray a 9" x 13" pan with non stick cooking spray. Arrange broccoli in pan and place chicken on top. In small bowl, combine soup, mayonnaise and lemon juice. Pour over chicken. Sprinkle with cheese. In a separate container, mix melted margarine into bread crumbs with a fork and sprinkle over the top of everything. Bake at 350° for 30 minutes.

*Do not follow where the path leads.
Rather, go where there is no path and leave a trail.*

CHICKEN SPAGHETTI

4 1/2 oz. cooked spaghetti
2 chicken breasts, cooked and cubed
3 oz. Velveeta Cheese, light

1/4 C. salsa
1 can cream of mushroom soup
1/2 C. finely chopped onion
8 oz. frozen broccoli

Cook spaghetti according to package directions. Lightly spray a skillet with non stick spray. Cook chicken in skillet until no longer pink in center. Remove from pan and cut into cubes. In the same pan, mix Velveeta with soup, onion and salsa, heat on medium. The cheese will melt without sticking. Cook broccoli in microwave according to package instructions. Mix all ingredients together. Pour into sprayed 9" X 13" pan. Cover and bake for approximately 20 minutes at 450° or until heated throughout. Serve immediately.

QUICK AND EASY CHICKEN POT PIE

1 pkg. chicken flavored stuffing mix
4 T. butter or margarine
1 1/2 C. hot water
1 jar chicken gravy or mushroom soup

2 C. chicken, cooked and cubed
1 pkg. frozen mixed vegetables, thawed & drained
1/4 tsp. dried thyme (optional)

Stir together contents of seasoning package (found in stuffing box), margarine and water, bring to boil. Remove from heat. Add stuffing crumbs stirring until water is absorbed. Spray a two quart casserole with non stick cooking spray. Mix gravy, chicken, veggies and thyme in casserole dish. Spoon stuffing over chicken mixture and cook on high in microwave for about 15 minutes. Makes 6 servings.

CHICKEN CASSEROLE

3 C. stuffing croutons
1 C. canned sliced mushrooms
3 C. chicken, cooked and cubed (leftover)
1/2 C. butter
1/2 C. flour
4 C. chicken broth
1 tsp. salt
1/2 tsp. pepper
6 eggs slightly beaten
Topping:
1 can cream of chicken soup
1/2 C. sour cream

In a large bowl, mix stuffing, mushrooms and chicken. Lightly spray a 9" x 13" pan with cooking spray. Spread mixture into prepared pan. Melt butter in a sauce pan, add flour to make a paste, then slowly add the chicken broth. Cook slightly till it thickens. Cool. Stir in eggs and pour over the chicken mixture. Bake at 325° for 45 minutes, let stand for 5 minutes before serving. In a small sauce pan, heat the soup and sour cream until well blended. Do not boil. Pour topping over casserole.

GRILLED TILAPIA

2-3 T. canola oil
6-8 cloves garlic, peeled and sliced
4-4 oz. tilapia fillets
1 tsp. Lawry's Seasoning Salt
1/2 tsp. ground black pepper

Heat oil in large skillet over medium high heat. Add sliced garlic and sauté until lightly browned. Move garlic to side of pan and add fish. Sprinkle with Lawry's and pepper. Cook for 2-3 minutes and turn fish. Place garlic pieces on top of fish and continue cooking until fish is translucent and flakes easily. Serves 4.

Just remember...if the world didn't suck, we'd all fall off.

CRAB QUESADILLAS

1 C. shredded Mexican cheese
1/2 C. mayonnaise
1/4 C. sour cream
6 oz. crab meat, flaked (or cooked, peeled shrimp)
1 1/2 T. sliced green onions
1 1/2 T. chopped green chilies
3-10" flour tortillas
Salsa, optional

In a medium bowl, combine cheese, mayonnaise, sour cream, crab meat, onions and chilies. Mix until well blended. Divide mixture evenly onto tortillas. Fold tortillas in half. Lightly spray a cookie sheet with non stick cooking spray and place filled tortillas on single layer. Bake at 425° for 7-10 minutes until cheese is melted. Remove from oven and let stand 2-3 minutes. Cut each tortilla into thirds and serve with salsa.

*If raising children was going to be easy,
it never would have started with something called labor!*

Desserts

RHUBARB CUSTARD PIE

Crust for 2 crust pie, 9", unbaked
3 eggs, slightly beaten
3 T. milk
2 C. sugar
1/4 C. flour
3/4 tsp. nutmeg
4 C. rhubarb, cut in 1/2" pieces
1 T. butter

Make pastry for 2 crust pie. Line a 9" pie pan with half of the dough. Beat eggs and milk until frothy. Mix flour, nutmeg, and sugar together, then add to egg mixture. Fold in the rhubarb. Pour into pie shell. Cut the butter into 4-5 pieces and dot the top of the pie. Gently place the top crust on the pie and seal the edges. Cut 3-4 slits in the top crust. Sprinkle top with a little sugar. Bake at 400° for 50-60 minutes.
NOTE: For a change of pace, replace 1 cup of the rhubarb with either sliced strawberries or blueberries.

BUTTERFINGER PIE

1-9" graham cracker pie crust
1-8 oz. pkg. cream cheese, softened
3 large size Butterfinger candy bars
8 oz. Cool Whip
Chocolate syrup (optional)

Prepare graham cracker crust and set aside. Beat cream cheese until fluffy. Crush candy bars, reserve about 1 T. for top. Add remaining crushed candy bars to cream cheese. Gently fold Cool Whip into cream cheese mixture. Pour into pie shell. Drizzle with chocolate syrup and sprinkle with reserved candy pieces. Refrigerate until ready to serve.
NOTE: You may also use other candy bars like; heath bars or snickers.

A fine is a tax for doing wrong.
A tax is a fine for doing well.

BUTTERSCOTCH PIE

1-9" baked pastry shell	4 T. butter
1 C. firmly packed brown sugar	1 1/2 tsp. vanilla
1/2 C. flour, or 4 T. cornstarch	4 egg whites
1/4 tsp. salt	1/4 tsp. cream of tartar
2 1/2 C. milk	1/2 tsp. vanilla
4 slightly beaten egg yolks	8 T. sugar

Blend sugar, flour, and salt in sauce pan. Over medium heat, gradually add milk. Cook and stir until mixture thickens and starts to boil. Cook for 2 minutes, stirring constantly. Remove from heat. Separate egg yolks and egg whites. Gradually add a small amount of the hot mixture to the beaten egg yolks. Then return the yolk mixture to the sauce pan. Cook for another 2 minutes, stirring constantly. Remove from heat. Stir in the butter and vanilla. Let cool to room temperature, stirring occasionally. Pour into pie shell. In a chilled mixer bowl, beat egg whites, cream of tartar, and vanilla until soft peaks form. Gradually add sugar, beating until stiff peaks form. Spread on top of butterscotch filling sealing to the edges. Bake at 350° for 12-15 minutes or until meringue is golden brown. Cool.

STREUSEL TOPPED PUMPKIN PIE

1-9" unbaked pie crust	1/4 tsp. salt
1-15 oz. canned pumpkin	1/4 C. packed brown sugar
1-12 oz. can evaporated milk	2 T. flour
1/2 C. sugar	2 T. butter or margarine
2 eggs, slightly beaten	1/2 C. chopped pecans
1 1/2 tsp. pumpkin pie spice	

Preheat oven to 425°. Prepare unbaked pie crust and set aside. Do not prick crust. In large bowl, combine pumpkin, milk, sugar, eggs, salt and spice. Mix well. Pour into crust and bake for 20 minutes. Reduce heat to 350° and bake for another 20 minutes. Meanwhile, mix the brown sugar, flour, butter and pecans with pastry blender. Sprinkle streusel ingredients over top of pumpkin filling and bake another 20 minutes or until knife inserted near center comes out clean. Cool completely. Store in refrigerator until ready to serve. Top with whipped cream, if desired.

PUMPKIN CHEESE PIE

1-9" graham cracker crust
4 oz. cream cheese, softened
1 T. milk
1 T. sugar
12 oz. Cool Whip
1 C. cold milk
1 can pumpkin
2-4 oz. pkgs. Instant vanilla pudding mix
1 tsp. cinnamon
1/2 tsp. ginger
1/4 tsp. cloves

Prepare graham cracker crust and set aside. Beat cream cheese, 1 T. milk and sugar in mixer until smooth. Fold in the Cool Whip. Pour into prepared crust. In a large bowl, combine 1 cup milk, pumpkin, pudding mix and spices. Beat with whisk until thickened. Spread over the cream cheese layer in pie shell. Refrigerate for at least 4 hours before serving.

PECAN PIE

1-9" unbaked pastry shell
1/4 C. butter or margarine, softened
1/2 C. sugar
1 C. dark corn syrup (Karo)
1/4 tsp. salt
3 eggs
1 C. pecans, coarsely chopped

Prepare pie crust and set aside. In a large bowl, cream butter. Add sugar and beat until fluffy. Blend in salt and syrup and mix well. Add eggs one at a time, beating well after each addition. Gently stir in pecans. Pour into the prepared pie shell. Bake at 350° for 50 minutes or until knife inserted near center comes out clean. Cool.

*When you get to the end of your rope,
tie a knot in it and hang on.*

COCONUT CREAM PIE

1-9" baked pastry shell
1 C. sugar
1/2 C. flour or 4 T. cornstarch
1/4 tsp. salt
2 1/2 C. milk
4 egg yolks, slightly beaten
2 1/2 T. butter or margarine

1 tsp. vanilla
1 1/3 C. coconut
4 egg whites
1/4 tsp. cream of tartar
1/2 tsp. vanilla
8 T. sugar

Prepare pie shell and set aside. Separate eggs. Combine sugar, flour and salt in sauce pan. Over medium heat, gradually add milk. Cook until mixture begins to boil and thicken, stirring constantly. Boil for 2 minutes. Remove from heat. Stir some of the hot mixture into the beaten egg yolks. Then add the yolks to the saucepan. Bring to a boil and continue cooking for another 2 minutes. Remove from heat. Add butter, 1 cup coconut and vanilla. Cool to room temperature, stirring occasionally. Pour into baked pastry shell. In a chilled mixer bowl, beat egg whites, cream of tartar, and vanilla until soft peaks form. Gradually add sugar, beating until stiff peaks form. Spread on top of coconut filling. Sprinkle remaining coconut on top of meringue. Bake at 350° for 12-15 minutes or until meringue is golden brown. Cool.

COCONUT FUDGE PIE

1 1/2 T. softened butter (almost melted)
2 C. coconut
1-12 oz. can evaporated milk
2/3 C. firmly packed brown sugar

1 egg
3 T. flour
1 tsp. vanilla
4-1 oz. squares semi sweet chocolate, melted

Coat the bottom and sides of a 9" pie pan with butter. Press 1 1/3 cups of coconut into pie pan to form a crust. Set aside. In mixer, combine milk, sugar, egg, flour, vanilla, and melted chocolate. Blend on high speed for about two minutes or until smooth. Pour into prepared pie pan. Sprinkle with remaining coconut. Bake at 325° for 30-35 minutes. Can be served warm or cold. Store in refrigerator.

FRESH RASPBERRY PIE

1-9" deep dish pie shell, baked
1-8 oz. pkg. cream cheese, softened
1 C. powdered sugar
8 oz. Cool Whip

2 C. fresh berries
1 1/2 cup water
3/4 C. sugar
1-3 oz. pkg. raspberry Jello
2 T. cornstarch

Prepare pie shell and set aside. Beat cream cheese and powdered sugar until fluffy. Fold in Cool Whip. Pour into pie shell. Arrange berries on top of filling. Cook water, sugar, Jello, and cornstarch until thickened and clear. Let cool a few minutes until it starts to set up, then pour over berries. Chill for 4 hours before serving.
NOTE: This pie can also be made with strawberries and strawberry Jello, or the recipe can be doubled and put into a 9" x 13" pan.

STRAWBERRY PIE

1-9" baked pie shell
1 C. sugar
3 T. cornstarch
1-12 oz. can of 7 Up

Red food coloring
1 pt. strawberries
1-2 tsp. sugar
Whipped cream (or Cool Whip)

Combine sugar and cornstarch in pan. Add 7 Up and stir until smooth. Cook over medium heat until the mixture starts to thicken. Cook for 1-2 minutes, then cool to room temperature. Add 1-3 drops of red food coloring.
Wash and slice strawberries. Carefully arrange the strawberries in pie shell and sprinkle with 1-2 tsp. of sugar. Pour the cooled 7 Up mixture over the strawberries. Refrigerate until set up. Serve with whipped cream.

WHIPPED STRAWBERRY CREAM PIE

1-9" chocolate crumb crust
4 C. fresh strawberries, divided
1-14 oz. can sweetened
    condensed milk

1/8 C. lemon juice
1-8 oz. container Cool whip

Prepare crumb crust and set aside. Mash 2 cups of the strawberries in a large bowl. Stir in condensed milk and juice. Gently fold in 2 cups of the Cool Whip. Pour into prepared crust. Cover and freeze at least 6 hours. Remove from freezer 10-15 minutes before serving. Frost with remaining Cool Whip. Slice the rest of the strawberries and carefully spread on top of Cool Whip.

CREAMY FROZEN LIME PIE

1-8" graham cracker crust
1-8 oz. pkg. cream cheese,
    softened
1-14 oz. can sweetened
    condensed milk

1 C. evaporated milk
1/2 C. lime juice (about 3
    medium limes)
1 tsp. grated lime peel
Lime slices, berries or mint sprigs

Prepare graham cracker crust and set aside. Beat cream cheese until smooth. Gradually add sweetened condensed milk and evaporated milk. Blend in lime juice and lime peel. Beat on medium speed for one minute. Pour into crust. Freeze for at least 2 hours or until firm. Let stand at room temperature for 10-15 minutes before serving. Garnish with lime slices, berries or mint sprigs.

PEANUT BUTTER PIE

2-8" graham cracker crusts
12 oz. cream cheese, softened
1 1/2 C. powdered sugar
3/4 C. peanut butter

3/4 C. milk
16 oz. Cool Whip
Chocolate syrup (optional)
Chopped peanuts (optional)

Prepare crumb crusts and set aside or buy ready made crusts. Blend cream cheese and sugar together. Add peanut butter and milk. Carefully fold in Cool Whip. Divide into the two pie shells. Cover and freeze. Remove from freezer 10 minutes before serving. Drizzle top of pie with thin stripes of chocolate syrup and sprinkle with chopped peanuts, if desired.

GRAHAM CRACKER CRUST

1 1/2 C. fine graham cracker crumbs
1/4 C. sugar
1/2 C. butter or margarine, melted

Mix crumbs and sugar. Add melted butter and stir with a fork. Press firmly into bottom and partially up the sides of a 9" spring form pan or a 9" pie pan. Bake at 375° for 8 minutes or until edges are slightly brown. Cool.

CHOCOLATE CRUMB CRUST

1 1/2 C. chocolate sandwich cookies, or chocolate graham crackers, or chocolate wafer cookies, crushed
1/4 C. sugar
1/2 C. butter or margarine, melted

Mix crumbs and sugar. Add melted butter and stir with a fork. Press firmly into bottom and partially up the sides of a 9" spring form pan or a 9" pie pan. Bake at 375° for 8 minutes or until edges are slightly brown. Cool.

SOUR CREAM CHEESECAKE

16 whole graham crackers, crushed
1/4 C. butter, melted
16 oz. creamed cottage cheese
1 1/3 C. sugar
3 eggs, beaten
1 1/3 T. lemon juice
1 1/3 tsp. vanilla
8 oz. sour cream
2 T. Sugar

Stir the crushed graham crackers and butter with a fork. Press into a 9" Spring form pan to form a crust. Bake at 375° for 5 minutes. Cool. In a separate bowl, cream cottage cheese, sugar, eggs, lemon juice and vanilla with electric mixer. Pour into prepared crust. Bake at 350° for 35-40 minutes. In a small bowl, mix together sour cream and sugar. Spread on top of hot cheesecake. Bake for another 5 minutes. Cool to room temperature, then refrigerate for at least 2 hours.
Cheesecake dates back to 800 BC. It was created in ancient Greece. The first Olympic athletes (in 776BC) were served cheesecake to keep up their strength and energy.

CHOCOLATE LOVERS CHEESECAKE

2-8 oz. pkgs. cream cheese, softened
1/2 C. sugar
1/2 tsp. vanilla

2 eggs
4-1 oz. squares semi sweet chocolate, melted
9" chocolate crumb crust

Prepare chocolate crumb crust and set aside. In mixer bowl, mix cream cheese, sugar and vanilla. Add eggs and melted chocolate. Blend well. Pour into prepared crust. Bake at 350° for 40 minutes or until center is almost set. Cool. Refrigerate at least 3 hours. Garnish with chocolate sauce and chocolate chips.

TOFFEE CHEESECAKE

1 pkg. (18 oz.) refrigerated oatmeal cookie dough with chocolate and butterscotch chips
2-8 oz. pkgs. cream cheese, softened

2 eggs
1/2 C. sugar
1 tsp. vanilla
4 Heath candy bars, coarsely chopped

Preheat oven to 350°. Slice cookie dough into 24 slices. (Cookie dough may be easier to slice if put in the freezer for 2-3 hours before using.) Arrange on the bottom and up the sides of a 9" deep dish pie plate or spring form pan, sprayed with cooking spray. Press the dough together making a uniform crust. Set aside. In a large bowl, using an electric mixer, beat cream cheese, eggs, sugar and vanilla for 1 minute until well mixed. Stir in candy pieces. Pour into lined pie plate. Bake for 40-45 minutes until the center is firm. Remove from oven and allow to cool. Cover loosely and chill for 4 hours or overnight.

QUICK AND EASY CHERRY CHEESECAKE

1-12 oz. can sweetened condensed milk
1/3 C. lemon juice
1-8 oz. pkg. cream cheese, softened

1 tsp. vanilla
1-9" graham cracker crust
1 can cherry pie filling

In electric mixer combine condensed milk, lemon juice, cream cheese, and vanilla. Mix well. Pour into graham cracker crust and chill. When firm, top with cherry pie filling. Doesn't get much easier that this.

CHOCOLATE CHIP CHEESECAKE BARS

1-18 oz pkg. chocolate chip cookie dough
1-8 oz. pkg. cream cheese, softened
1/3 C. sugar
1 egg
1 T. Instant coffee crystals
1 tsp. water
1 tsp. vanilla
1/2 C. mini semi sweet chocolate pieces

Crumble cookie dough in a 9" x 13" pan. Press evenly onto bottom of pan. Set aside. Beat cream cheese, sugar, and egg together until smooth. In a small bowl, mix coffee, water and vanilla until crystals are dissolved. Stir coffee mixture into cheese mixture, then spread evenly over crust. Sprinkle with chocolate pieces. Bake at 350° for 20 minutes or until set. Cool completely in pan on wire rack. Cut into bars.

PUMPKIN CHEESECAKE BARS

2 C. gingersnaps, finely crushed (about 30)
1/4 C. butter or margarine, melted
1/3 C. canned pumpkin
1 T. flour
1 tsp. pumpkin pie spice
3-8 oz. pkgs. cream cheese, softened
1 C. sugar
1 1/2 tsp. vanilla
3 eggs

Lightly grease (or spray) a 9" x 13" pan. Combine gingersnaps and melted butter in small bowl, stir with a fork. Press into bottom of prepared pan. Bake at 325° about 10 minutes. Cool. In a medium bowl, combine pumpkin, flour, and pumpkin pie spice. Set aside. In a large bowl, beat cream cheese until smooth. Add sugar and vanilla. Stir in eggs, one at a time, beating after each. Take one third of cream cheese batter and blend it into pumpkin mixture until smooth. Pour remaining cream cheese batter over crust, spreading evenly. Place large spoonfuls of pumpkin batter over cheesecake layer. Swirl together with knife, being careful not disturb crust. Bake at 325° for 25-30 minutes until center is set. Cool. Cover and chill for 4 hours before cutting.

BLUEBERRY TORTE

1/2 lb. graham crackers, crushed fine
1 stick butter or margarine, melted
3/4 C. sugar
1-8 oz. pkg. cream cheese, softened
1 C. powdered sugar
1 tsp. vanilla
12 oz. Cool Whip
1 can blueberry pie filling

Combine graham cracker crumbs and 3/4 C. sugar. Using a fork, stir in melted butter. Press firmly into the bottom of a 9" x 13" pan. Beat together cream cheese and powdered sugar, adding sugar a little at a time. Add vanilla. Fold in Cool Whip. Pour evenly into crust in pan. Top with the blueberry pie filling. Cover and refrigerate overnight.

CHERRY SURPRISE

20 squares graham crackers, crushed
1/4 C. butter, melted
1 pt. whipping cream
1/2 tsp. vanilla
2 T. sugar
2 C. mini marshmallows
1 can cherry pie filling

Stir graham crackers crumbs and butter together with a fork and pat into 9" x 13" pan. (save 1/4 cup crumbs for top). Whip cream and vanilla until stiff. Add sugar a little at a time, then add marshmallows. Put half of cream mixture over graham cracker crust. Spread cherries over cream. Add the remaining cream mixture and sprinkle with reserved crumbs. Chill several hours or overnight.

Holding a grudge is letting someone live rent free in your head.

COCONUT CREAM DESSERT

1 C. flour
1/2 C. pecans, finely chopped
4 oz. butter, softened
8 oz. cream cheese
1 C. powered sugar
8 oz. carton of cool whip

2-3 oz. pkgs. instant coconut cream pudding
(lemon or chocolate may be used)
2 1/2 C. milk
1/4 C. pecans, chopped

Stir flour and finely chopped pecans together. Cut butter into flour mixture and press firmly into greased 9" x 13" pan. Bake at 350° for 10 minutes. Cool. Mix cream cheese and powered sugar together. Fold in 1 C. cool whip. Spread onto baked crust. In a separate bowl, beat pudding and milk with whisk until it thickens, then pour over creamy mixture. Spread remainder of cool whip on top. Sprinkle 1/4 cup chopped pecans on top.

POLISH DRUMSTICKS

2 C. vanilla wafers, crushed
4 oz. butter or margarine, melted
2/3 C. peanuts, chopped (dry roasted)
8 oz. cream cheese
1/3 C. peanut butter
1 C. powdered sugar

4 C. cool whip
3 C. milk
2 small packages instant chocolate pudding
1/3 C. peanuts, chopped fine (dry roasted)
1 Hershey bar

Combine wafers, butter and chopped peanuts with fork and pat into a lightly greased 9" x 13" pan. Bake at 350° for 10 minutes. Cool. In separate bowl, beat cream cheese, peanut butter and powdered sugar until smooth. Fold in 2 cups cool whip. Spread over crust. Beat pudding and milk until thickened. Spread on cream cheese layer. Spread 2 cups cool whip on top of pudding. Sprinkle 1/3 cup of fine chopped peanuts on top. Grate Hershey bar on top. Refrigerate.

WAVERLY TORT

40 Waverly crackers, crushed
4 oz. butter, softened
4 egg whites
1 cup sugar
1 can lemon pie filling

2 T. Lemon juice
Grated rind of 1 lemon
1 pint whipping cream
1-2 tsp. sugar

Combine crackers and butter. Mix with pastry blender like pie crust, pat into bottom of 9" x 13" pan. Beat egg whites till stiff. Add sugar gradually and beat well. Spread over crumbs and bake at 350° for 15 minutes. Cool. Mix pie filling with lemon juice and grated lemon rind. Spread on cooked meringue. Whip whipping cream, adding 1-2 tsp. sugar gradually, and spread on top of lemon filing. Refrigerate overnight.

ANGEL TORTE

3/4 of a larger (purchased) Angel food cake
8 oz. butter or margarine
1 C. powder sugar
4 large egg yolks

2 tsp. vanilla
1 pt. whipping cream, whipped
4 butter finger candy bars, crushed
1/2 C. pecans, chopped

Line the bottom or a 9" x 13" pan with 1/2 of the Angel food cake broken into small pieces. Mix butter, sugar, vanilla, and egg yolks, beating well. Blend into whipping cream that has been whipped. Spread 1/2 of the mixture over cake pieces in pan. Crush candy bars and spread 1/2 of them over mixture. Repeat layers of cake pieces, sauce, candy bars and top with pecans. Refrigerate overnight or for several hours.

Happiness is like jam.
You can't spread even a little without getting some on yourself.

CHEESE DANISH

2 pkgs. Crescent Rolls
2-8 oz. pkgs. cream cheese, softened
1 C. sugar
1 tsp. vanilla
1 egg, separated
1/4 C. sugar
1/4 C. pecans, chopped (or walnuts)

Open 1 pkg. Crescent Rolls and spread in bottom of a 9" x 13" pan. Stretch to fit and seal holes. In mixer bowl, beat cream cheese, sugar, vanilla, and egg yolk until smooth. Spread over unbaked rolls. Cover with remaining pkg. of rolls. (To do this, spread Crescent rolls on bread board, then carefully lift and place on cheese mixture.) Beat egg white until frothy and spread on top of crescent layer. Sprinkle with 1/4 cup sugar and nuts. Bake at 350° for 25-30 minutes. Cool to room temperature. Chill in refrigerator. Cut in 2" squares.

APPLE SLICES

3 C. flour
2 tsp. baking powder
1/4 C. sugar
Pinch of salt
8 oz. butter or margarine, softened
1 egg beaten
1/2 C. water
6 to 8 C. peeled sliced apples
1 T. cinnamon
3/4 C. sugar

Mix flour, baking powder, 1/4 cup sugar, salt and butter with a pastry blender like pie crust. Add egg and water. Roll half of dough for bottom of a jelly roll pan. Fill with apple slices. Sprinkle cinnamon and 3/4 cup sugar over apples. Roll remainder of dough and lay on top. Bake at 350° for 1 hour. Frost with powdered sugar frosting when cool.

There isn't any map on the road to success; you have to find your own way.

FRENCH LEMON BARS

1 1/2 C. flour, sifted
1/3 C. powdered sugar
6 oz. butter or margarine
1 1/2 C. sugar

1 T. flour
3 eggs, beaten
3 T. lemon juice
Powdered sugar

Combine flour and powdered sugar together. Cut butter in with pastry blender. Press into 9" x 13" pan. Bake at 350° for 20 minutes. Mix 1 T. flour and 1 1/2 C. sugar together. Stir into eggs by hand. Add lemon juice. Pour filling onto hot crust. Bake at 350° for 20 minutes more. Dust with powdered sugar.

PUMPKIN CRUNCH

1 can (16 oz) pumpkin
1 can (12 oz) evaporated milk
3 eggs, beaten
1 1/2 C. sugar
4 tsp. pumpkin pie spice

1 1/2 tsp. salt
1 pkg. yellow cake mix
1 C. pecan, chopped
16 oz. butter or margarine, melted

Combine pumpkin, evaporated milk, eggs, sugar, pumpkin pie spice and salt in a large bowl. Pour into a greased 9" x 13" pan. Spread dry cake mix evenly over pumpkin mix. Top with pecans. Drizzle melted butter over top. Bake at 350° for 50 to 55 minutes. Cool completely. Serve with whipped cream.

He who laughs last, thinks slowest.

PUMPKIN BARS

2 C. sugar
1 C. canola oil
2 eggs, beaten
16 oz. canned pumpkin
2 C. flour, sifted
1 tsp. baking soda
2 tsp. baking powder
1 tsp. salt

2 tsp. cinnamon
Frosting:
3/4 stick butter or margarine
8 oz. cream cheese
1 T. milk
1 tsp. vanilla
2 1/2 C. powdered sugar
1 C. walnuts, chopped (optional)

Mix sugar, oil, eggs, and pumpkin in electric mixer. In a separate bowl, sift dry ingredients together. Gradually add to egg mixture and beat until well mixed. Pour into 2 well greased and floured 9" x 13" pans. Bake at 350° for 30 minutes. Cool. For frosting, cream butter, cream cheese, milk and vanilla. Add powdered sugar gradually. Beat until smooth. Frost both cakes. Sprinkle nuts on top if desired.

RHUBARB DREAM BARS

CRUST:
2 T. sugar
2 C. flour
1 C. butter or margarine
FILLING:
5 C. rhubarb, diced
2 C. sugar

1/4 tsp. salt
4 egg yolks
1 C. evaporated milk
TOPPING:
4 egg whites
2 tsp. vanilla
8 T. Sugar

Combine flour and sugar. Cut in butter with pastry blender. Press into a 9" x 13" pan. Bake at 350° for 10 minutes. Mix rhubarb, sugar, salt, egg yolks and milk together thoroughly. Spread on partially baked crust. Bake for another 40-50 minutes. In chilled mixer bowl, whip egg whites and vanilla until soft peaks form. Gradually add sugar and whip until stiff peaks form. Spread on top of bars and bake for 8-10 more minutes or until golden brown. Cool.

RHUBARB COBBLER

4 C. rhubarb, diced
3/4 C. sugar
1 small pkg. strawberry Jello

1 pkg. white or yellow cake mix
1 1/2 C. water
1 stick butter or margarine

Lightly spray a 9" x 13" pan with cooking spray. Spread cut up rhubarb evenly on bottom of pan. Mix sugar and Jello together and sprinkle on fruit. Layer dry cake mix on top of fruit/sugar layer. Pour water gently across all. Cut butter into thin slices and place evenly on top of everything. Bake at 350° for 45 minutes.
NOTE: Other fruits can be used in combination with other flavors of Jello, such as; peaches and peach Jello; apples and lemon Jello; raspberries and raspberry Jello.

RHUBARB CAKE

1 1/2 C. sugar
4 oz. butter, softened
1 egg, beaten
1 tsp. vanilla
1 C. buttermilk
2 C. flour

1/2 tsp. salt
1 tsp. baking soda
2 to 3 C. rhubarb, raw, chopped
1/2 C. sugar
1 tsp. cinnamon

Cream sugar and butter together, add egg, vanilla and buttermilk. In a separate bowl sift flour, salt and baking soda together. Gradually add to the creamed mixture. Fold in the rhubarb. Pour into a greased 9" x 13" pan. Mix 1/2 cup sugar and cinnamon, sprinkle over dough. Bake at 350° for 50 minutes.

Children are like wet cement.
Whatever falls on them makes an impression.

FRUIT COFFEE CAKE

2 T. sugar
2 T. butter or margarine, softened
1 egg, slightly beaten
3 oz. milk
1 C. flour
1 tsp. baking powder
1/2 tsp. salt
4 C. rhubarb, chopped, or any other fruit
(Drain if canned)

TOPPING:
1/2 C. sugar
1/2 C. brown sugar
1/2 C. flour
2 T. butter or margarine

In a bowl, mix sugar, butter, egg and milk. In a separate bowl, sift together flour, baking powder and salt. Add to creamed mixture. Spread the mix in a 9" x 13" ungreased pan. Spread the fruit on top of the dough. For the topping, mix the sugars and flour together, cut in the butter with a pastry blender. Sprinkle the topping over the fruit. Bake at 350° for 30 to 35 minutes.

FRUIT PIZZA

18 oz pkg. refrigerated sugar cookie dough
8 oz. cream cheese, softened
1/3 C. sugar
1/2 tsp. vanilla
Suggested fruits: mandarin orange, strawberries, green grapes, purple grapes, bananas or blueberries

Slice cookie dough in 1/8" slices and place on pizza pan overlapping slightly. Press together lightly. Bake at 375° for 12 to 15 minutes. Cool. Beat cream cheese with sugar and vanilla. Spread it onto cooled cookie shell. Arrange fruit on top of cream cheese. Chill. If you use bananas, put them on just before serving.

DUMP CAKE

1 can (20 oz.) crushed pineapple in syrup
1 can (21 oz.) cherry pie filling
1 pkg. yellow cake mix
1 C. pecans, chopped
1 stick (4 oz.) margarine or butter, cut thin

Lightly spray a 9" x 13" pan. Spread the pineapple evenly in it. Dump in the pie filling and spread evenly. Dump cake mix in and spread out. Sprinkle pecans on top. Dot butter on top. Bake at 350° for 48 to 53 minutes.

BETTER THAN SEX CAKE

1 1/2 C. graham cracker crumbs
1 C. walnuts, chopped
1 tsp. cinnamon
1/2 C. butter or margarine, melted
1-8 oz. pkg. cream cheese, softened
3/4 C. sugar
8 oz. Cool Whip
1 small pkg. instant vanilla pudding
1 small pkg. instant chocolate or butterscotch or other flavored pudding
3 C. milk
8 oz. Cool Whip

Combine graham cracker crumbs, walnuts and cinnamon. Stir in butter with fork. Press into the bottom of a 9" x 13" pan. (Save a little to sprinkle on top.) Bake at 350° for 10 minutes. Cool. Beat cream cheese and sugar until smooth. Fold in Cool Whip and spread on cooled crust. Mix the two puddings mixes together and add milk. Using a wire whisk, stir until pudding thickens. Pour over cheese mixture. Spread the 8 oz. of Cool Whip on top. Sprinkle with reserved graham cracker crumbs. Cover and refrigerate until ready to serve.

DIRT CAKE

1 large pkg. Oreo cookies
3 small pkgs. instant chocolate pudding mix
4 1/2-5 C. milk
1-8 oz. pkg. cream cheese, softened
16 oz. Cool Whip
1-8" diameter, clean plastic flower pot

Crush the Oreo cookies in a blender or food processor. Set aside. In a large bowl, mix the milk and pudding mix with wire whisk until thickened. In a separate bowl, beat the cream cheese. Blend in the pudding mixture. Fold in the Cool Whip. Layer cookie crumbs and pudding mixture alternately in flower pot, starting and ending with cookie crumbs. Insert a bunch of clean plastic flowers and some Gummi worms if desired. Serve with a new, clean trowel.

PINEAPPLE UPSIDE DOWN CAKE (THE WAY MOM MADE IT IN THE 50'S)

1/2 C. butter
1 C. brown sugar
1 #2 can sliced pineapple
2 T. large whole pecans
1 C. flour
1 tsp. baking powder
1/8 tsp. salt
3 eggs, separated
1 C. sugar
5 T. pineapple juice

Melt butter in a 9" x 9" baking pan. (A 10" cast iron skillet would be perfect if you have one.) Spread brown sugar evenly in pan. Arrange the pineapple slices in one layer on the brown sugar, filling in spaces with pecans. Sift the flour, baking powder and salt into a mixing bowl. Set aside. Beat egg yolks in a separate bowl until light, adding sugar gradually. Add pineapple juice and sifted flour. In a chilled bowl, beat the egg whites until stiff peaks form. Fold stiffly beaten egg whites into batter. Pour batter over pineapple slices in pan. Bake at 375° for 30 to 35 minutes. Place cake plate upside down over cake, turn everything over and remove pan. Serve with whipped cream if desired.

ZUCCHINI CAKE

2 1/2 C. flour, sifted
1/2 tsp. salt
1 1/2 tsp. cinnamon
1/2 tsp. baking soda
1/2 tsp, baking powder
1 C. canola oil
2 C. sugar
4 eggs, beaten
2 C. zucchini, shredded
1/2 C. walnuts, chopped
   (optional)

FROSTING:
3 oz. cream cheese, softened
1/4 C. butter or margarine,
   softened
1 T. milk
1 tsp. vanilla
2 C. powered sugar
1/4 C. walnuts, chopped
   (optional)

In a mixing bowl, sift together flour, salt, cinnamon, baking soda and baking powder. In a separate bowl, combine oil, sugar and eggs. Gradually add the dry ingredients and mix well. Add zucchini and stir until thoroughly combined. Fold in walnuts if desired. Pour into a greased 9" x 13" pan. Bake at 350° for 35 to 40 minutes. Cool.
Mix frosting in a small bowl. Beat cream cheese, butter, milk and vanilla till smooth. Add powered sugar and mix well. Frost cake. Sprinkle with nuts if desired. Store in refrigerator. Makes 20 to 24 servings.

CHOCOLATE ZUCCHINI CAKE

1/2 C. butter or margarine,
   softened
1/2 C. canola oil
1 3/4 C. sugar
2 eggs, beaten
1 tsp. vanilla
1/2 C. sour milk
2 1/2 C. flour
4 T. cocoa

1/2 tsp. baking powder
1 tsp. baking soda
1 tsp. salt
2 C. zucchini, peeled &
   shredded
1/2 C. chocolate chips
1/2 C. chopped nuts
Note: To make sour milk add 1
   tsp. lemon juice or vinegar to
   1/2 C. milk.

In electric mixer, cream butter, oil and sugar. Add eggs, vanilla and milk. In a separate bowl, sift flour, cocoa, baking powder, baking soda and salt. Gradually add dry ingredients into creamed mixture. Beat well. Blend in zucchini. Spoon into a lightly greased and floured 9" x 13" pan. Sprinkle chocolate chips and nuts on top. Bake at 350° for 40 - 45 minutes.

COCOA COLA CAKE

2 C. flour
2 C. sugar
1 C. butter or margarine
3 T. baking cocoa
1 C. cola soda
1/2 C. buttermilk
2 eggs, beaten
1 tsp. baking soda

1 tsp. vanilla
1 1/2 C. mini marshmallows
FROSTING:
1 C. butter or margarine
3 T. cocoa
6 T. cola soda
2 C. powdered sugar
1 C. pecans or walnuts

In a large bowl, stir the flour and sugar together. In a sauce pan, heat the cocoa, butter and cola until it comes to a full boil. Add to the flour/sugar mixture, stirring thoroughly. Blend in buttermilk, eggs, baking soda, vanilla, and marshmallows. Spray a 9" x 13" pan with cooking spray. Pour batter into pan (it will be thin). Bake at 350° for 30-35 minutes. Meanwhile, make frosting. In a sauce pan, heat the butter, cocoa, and cola to a full boil. Remove from heat and add sugar beating well. Add nuts and spread over hot cake.

CARROT CAKE

4 eggs, beaten
2 C. sugar
1 1/2 C. canola oil
3 C. flour, sifted
2 tsp. cinnamon
2 tsp. baking soda
3 tsp. baking powder
1/2 tsp. salt

2 C. carrots, grated
3/4 C. walnuts, chopped
FROSTING:
3 oz. cream cheese
2 oz. butter
1 C. powdered sugar
1 tsp. vanilla

Mix eggs, sugar and oil together. In a separate bowl, sift together flour, cinnamon, baking soda, baking powder and salt. Add to egg mixture. Mix in nuts and carrots. Place into greased and floured tube pan. Bake at 350° for 1 1/4 hours. Cool in pan for 10 to 15 minutes. Loosen cake from pan with knife, invert pan on cake plate and remove pan. For frosting, combine cream cheese, butter and vanilla. Add sugar gradually. Beat till smooth. Spread frosting over cake.

APPLE CAKE

2 C. sugar
1 1/2 C. canola oil
1 tsp. vanilla
2 eggs, beaten
3 C. apples, diced
1 C. pecans or walnuts, chopped

3 C. flour
1 tsp. baking soda
1 tsp. salt
1 tsp. cinnamon

Blend sugar, oil, vanilla and eggs in a large mixing bowl. Stir the apples and nuts into the mixture. In a separate bowl, sift the flour, baking soda, salt and cinnamon together. Add to the apple mixture. Pour into a lightly greased and floured 9" x 13" pan. Bake at 350° for 45 minutes.

LEMON BERRY TRIFLE

1 large angel food cake, cut into cubes
1-16 oz. container lemon yogurt
1 small pkg. instant lemon pudding mix

8 oz. Cool Whip
Strawberries, raspberries, and/or blueberries

Cube angel food cake and set aside. In a medium bowl, whisk together yogurt and pudding mix until smooth. Fold in Cool Whip. In a trifle bowl or a clear glass bowl, layer half of the cake, half of the yogurt mixture and half of the berries. Repeat the layers, arranging fruit artistically on top.
NOTE: This very impressive dessert can also be made in individual serving sizes.

People, who do things that count, never stop to count them.

Cookies & Candies

MOM'S CHOCOLATE CHIP COOKIES

1 C. butter or margarine
3/4 C. white sugar
3/4 C. dark brown sugar
2 eggs, beaten
1 tsp. vanilla
2 tsp. hot water

2 C. plus 4 T. sifted all purpose flour
1 tsp. salt
1 tsp. baking soda
1 C. walnuts, chopped
1-12 oz. pkg. chocolate chips

Cream butter and sugars together. Add eggs, hot water and vanilla. In a separate bowl, sift flour, salt and baking soda together. Gradually add to creamed mixture. Add walnuts and chips and mix well. Drop by spoonfuls unto ungreased cookie sheet. Bake at 375° for 10-12 minutes.

SANDIES

1 C. butter
1/4 C. powdered sugar
2 tsp. vanilla
1 T. Water

2 C. flour
1 C. pecans, chopped
Powdered sugar

Cream butter, sugar, vanilla and water in mixer. Add flour and mix well. Blend in pecans. Form into small rolls (1 1/2" long), using about one heaping teaspoon of dough for each cookie. Place on ungreased cookie sheet about 2" apart. Bake at 300° for 20 minutes. While still hot, roll in powdered sugar. Makes about 3 dozen.

Light travels faster than sound.
This is why some people appear bright until you hear them speak.

BUFFALO CHIPS

1 C. butter or margarine, softened
1 C. canola oil
2 C. white sugar
2 C. brown sugar
4 eggs
2 tsp. vanilla
3 C. flour

1 tsp. salt
2 tsp. baking soda
2 tsp. baking powder
3 C. quick cooking oatmeal
1 C. walnuts or pecans, chopped
1-12 oz. pkg. chocolate chips

Cream butter, oil, and sugars in mixer bowl. Add eggs and vanilla, continue mixing until well blended. Sift flour, salt, baking soda and baking powder together in a separate bowl. With mixer at low speed, gradually add dry ingredients to creamed mixture. Scrape sides of bowl often. Add oatmeal, nuts and chips. Mix well. Batter is very generous. If dough is too moist, add more flour. Using a 1/3 cup measuring cup, drop dough onto ungreased cookie sheet. This makes a large (5"-6") cookie. To make a smaller cookie, use a tablespoon to drop dough. Bake at 350° for about 12 minutes. Cool on cookie sheet for 5-7 minutes. (I used to make these cookies for my college student sons. About 8-10 cookies fit in a 3 lb. coffee can.)

COCONUT OATMEAL COOKIES

1 C. butter or margarine
1 C. sugar
1 C. brown sugar
2 eggs
1 tsp. vanilla
1 tsp. salt

2 tsp. baking soda
1 tsp. baking powder
2 C. flour
2 C. quick oatmeal
2 C. coconut

Cream butter and sugars together. Add eggs, one at a time, mixing well after each. Add vanilla. In a separate bowl, sift the salt, baking soda, baking powder, and flour together. With the mixer at low speed, gradually add the flour. Scrape the sides of the bowl. Add the coconut and the oatmeal slowly, mixing well. Batter will be thick. Drop by teaspoon onto ungreased cookie sheet. Bake at 375° for 12-14 minutes. Do not over bake.

AMISH SUGAR COOKIES

1 C. butter or margarine
1 C. oil
1 C. white sugar
1 C. powdered sugar
2 eggs
1 tsp. vanilla
4 1/2 C. sifted flour
1 tsp. cream of tartar
1 tsp salt
1 tsp. baking soda

Combine sugars, butter and oil, beat well. Add eggs and vanilla and beat until fluffy. In a separate bowl, sift flour, cream of tartar, salt and baking soda together. Slowly add to creamed mixture. Drop by heaping teaspoons onto ungreased cookie sheet. If desired, press to flatten using a lightly floured glass. Bake at 350° for 10-12 minutes. While still hot, shake a cinnamon sugar mixture over the cookies. Makes 80-100 cookies.

KISSES IN THE DARK

6 oz. chocolate chips
3 egg whites
1/2 tsp. vanilla
1 C. sugar
1/3 C. crushed saltine crackers

Melt chocolate chips and cool slightly. In mixer bowl, beat the egg whites and vanilla until stiff. Gradually beat in sugar until very stiff. Fold in the crackers and cooled chocolate. Drop by tsp. on greased cookie sheet. Bake at 350° for 10-12 minutes. Remove cookies immediately. Makes about 4 dozen cookies.

GINGERSNAPS

3/4 C. butter or margarine
1 C. brown sugar
1/4 cup molasses
1 egg
2 1/4 C. flour
2 tsp. baking soda
1/2 tsp. salt
1 tsp. ginger
1 tsp. cinnamon
1/2 tsp. cloves

Cream butter, sugar, molasses, and egg together. In a separate bowl, sift flour, baking soda, salt, ginger, cinnamon and cloves together. Gradually add dry ingredients to creamed mixture. Form into small 1" diameter balls. Roll in granulated sugar. Place 2" apart on lightly sprayed cookie sheet. Bake at 375° for 10 minutes. Cool slightly before removing from pan. Makes about 5 dozen.

MOLASSES COOKIES

1 C. shortening or margarine	1 tsp. baking soda
1 C. white sugar	2 tsp. cinnamon
2 eggs	2 tsp. cloves
1 C. molasses	1/2 tsp. nutmeg
1 C. cold water	1 tsp. salt
4 C. flour	

Cream shortening and sugar. Beat in eggs. In a separate bowl, blend the molasses with the water, beating until creamed. In another separate bowl, sift flour, baking soda, cinnamon, cloves, nutmeg and salt together. Blend into creamed mixture alternately with molasses mixture. Beat only enough to mix dough. Drop by spoonful onto ungreased cookie sheet. Bake at 375° for 15 minutes.

BIG MAC COOKIES

2 T. margarine	1 box Vanilla Wafers
3 C. powdered sugar	1 box Thin Mints
2 tsp. milk	2 T. Sesame seeds
Food coloring, red, yellow, green	1 egg white
1/2 C. shredded coconut	

Mix two different containers of powdered sugar frosting using 1 Tblsp. Margarine, 1 tsp. milk, and 1 1/2 cup powdered sugar (approximately) each. To one container, add a few drops of red food coloring. This will become the ketchup. To another, add a few drops of yellow food coloring. This will become the mustard. Put the coconut in a third container with a tight fitting lid. Add a few drops of green food coloring, put the lid on tight and shake a few times. This one should look like shredded lettuce. For each cookie you will need 2 vanilla wafers and 1 thin mint. On the bottom of one cookie, spread yellow frosting. Sprinkle a little coconut around the outer edge. Add a thin mint. Spread red ketchup on bottom of second cookie and place frosting side down on mint. Brush top with a little egg white and sprinkle with sesame seeds. This is a fun little version of the Big Mac and easy enough for the kids to help.

STARLIGHT MINT SURPRISE COOKIES

1 C. butter or margarine
1 C. sugar
1/2 C. packed brown sugar
2 eggs
1 tsp. vanilla
1 T. Water

3 C. flour
1 tsp. baking soda
1/2 tsp. salt
1 pkg. chocolate mint wafers (flat 3/4" diameter)
Walnut halves

Cream butter and sugars. Add eggs, vanilla, and water and mix thoroughly. In a separate bowl, sift flour, baking soda and salt. Gradually add to creamed mixture. Cover and chill at least 2 hours. Enclose each wafer in about 1 T. of chilled dough. Place on greased cookie sheet, 2" apart. Top each cookie with a walnut half. Bake at 375° for 10-12 minutes. Makes about 4 1/2 dozen.

SEVEN LAYER BARS

1/2 C. butter, melted
1 1/2 C. graham cracker crumbs
1 C. semi sweet chocolate chips
1 C. butterscotch chips

1 C. walnuts, chopped
1-14 oz. Eagle Brand sweetened condensed milk
1 C. shredded coconut

Preheat oven to 350°. In a 10" x 15" jelly roll pan, melt butter. Layer ingredients in order given. Sprinkle graham crackers, chocolate chips, butterscotch chips, and walnuts evenly in pan. Pour sweetened condensed milk over all. Top with coconut. Press gently. Bake for 25 minutes or until golden brown. Cool. Cut into 2" x 2" squares.

A person is not old until regrets take the place of dreams.

BUTTERY OATMEAL TURTLE BARS

1 C. flour
1 C. rolled oats
3/4 C. brown sugar
1/2 C. butter, softened
1 1/2 C. whole pecans.

Caramel Topping:
1/2 C. butter
2/3 C. packed brown sugar
1/2 tsp. vanilla
8 oz. sweet baking chocolate

Combine flour, oats and brown sugar. Cut in butter with pastry blender. Pat firmly into 9" x 13" ungreased pan. Sprinkle with pecans. For topping, combine butter and sugar in heavy saucepan and cook over medium heat stirring constantly until entire surface is boiling. Boil for 1 minute and remove from heat, add vanilla. Pour evenly over pecans and crust. Bake at 350° until caramel is bubbly, about 15 to 18 minutes. Break chocolate into small chunks and sprinkle evenly over caramel layer. Bake 1 minute longer to allow chocolate to melt. Swirl chocolate for a marbled effect. Cool slightly, then chill to set chocolate. Cut into bars. Makes 4 to 5 dozen.

FRUIT BARS

1 C. butter or margarine, softened
1 3/4 C. sugar
4 eggs
1 tsp. vanilla
3 C. flour
1 1/2 tsp. baking powder

1/2 tsp. salt
1 can pie filling of your choice
FROSTING:
2 T. butter or margarine
1 tsp. vanilla
1-1 1/2 C. powdered sugar

Cream butter with sugar. Add eggs one at a time beating well after each one. Add vanilla. In separate bowl, sift flour, baking powder and salt together. Gradually add to egg mixture. Spread 2/3 batter evenly on a lightly sprayed 10" x 15" jelly roll pan. Spread the pie filling evenly on top of the batter. Drop the rest of batter by spoon on top. Bake at 350° for 30 minutes. Cool for 20 minutes before frosting. Cream 2 tablespoons of butter with vanilla. Add powdered sugar and beat until smooth. Drizzle powdered sugar frosting on top while warm.

BOAT BARS

3/4 C. white syrup
3/4 C. sugar
1 C. peanut butter, smooth or crunchy

2 C. Special K cereal
2 C. Rice Krispies
6 oz. chocolate chips, 12 oz. for a thicker topping

Heat syrup and sugar to dissolve sugar (do not boil). Microwave peanut butter about 1 1/2 minutes then add to syrup, stir well. Add Special K and Rice Krispies. Spread into a greased 9" x 13" pan. Melt chocolate chips and spread it on top. Let stand in a cool place to set. Cut into bars.

KIT KAT BARS

8 oz. butter
1/2 C. sugar
1 C. brown sugar
1/2 C. milk
2 C. graham crackers, crushed

1 box Waverly crackers
Topping:
1/2 C. chocolate chips
1/2 C. butterscotch chips
2/3 C. peanut butter

Boil butter, sugar, brown sugar, milk and graham crackers for 3 minutes. Cool. Put a layer of Waverly crackers on the bottom of a 9" x 13" pan. Pour 1/2 of sauce over crackers. Place another layer of crackers. Pour remainder of sauce over crackers. Chill slightly. To make topping, melt chocolate and butterscotch chips along with peanut butter. Pour topping over sauce. Refrigerate.

You can only be young once, but you can be immature forever.

CARAMEL NUT BROWNIES

14 oz. pkg. of caramels, unwrapped
2/3 C. evaporated milk
1 German chocolate cake mix

6 oz. butter, melted
1 C. chocolate chips
1 C. pecans, chopped

Melt caramels with 1/3 cup evaporated milk in the top of a double boiler barely simmering water. Stir frequently. Set aside. Combine cake mix with melted butter and remaining 1/3 cup evaporated milk. Spread half of this mixture into a greased 9" x 13" pan. Bake at 350° for 6 to 8 minutes. Remove from oven and sprinkle with chocolate chips and pecans. Drizzle caramel over chips and nuts. Cover with remaining cake batter. Continue baking at 350° for 15 minutes until brownies are firm to the touch. Cool before cutting. Makes 3 to 4 dozen.

BLACK FOREST BROWNIE BARS

1 pkg. (21.5 oz.) fudge brownie mix
1-8 oz. pkg. cream cheese, softened
1 can (14 oz.) sweetened condensed milk

2 tsp. vanilla
1 egg
1 can (21 oz.) cherry pie filling

Heat oven to 350°. Prepare brownie mix as directed on package, except bake only 20 minutes. Beat cream cheese, milk, vanilla and egg in bowl until smooth. Pour over partially baked brownie layer. Bake for another 25 minutes or until topping is set. Cool for 2 hours. Spread pie filling over top. Cut into 2" squares. Store in refrigerator. Makes 24 large or 48 small bars.

Excellence is never an accident.

CHOCOLATE MINT STICKS

2 eggs, beaten
4 oz. butter, melted
1 C. sugar
2 oz. unsweetened chocolate, melted
1/2 tsp. peppermint flavoring
1/2 C. flour, sifted
1/2 C. walnuts, chopped

Frosting:
2 T. butter
1 T. milk
1 C. powdered sugar
1 tsp. peppermint flavoring
A few drops of green food coloring
Chocolate topping:
1 oz. unsweetened chocolate
1 T. butter

Combine eggs, sugar and butter, mix well. Add melted chocolate and peppermint. Blend in flour and walnuts. Pour into greased 9" x 9" pan. Bake at 350° for 25 to 30 minutes. Cool. Make frosting by thoroughly mixing 2 T. butter, 1 T. milk, powdered sugar, 1 tsp. peppermint flavoring and a few drops of green food coloring. Spread on brownie layer. Chill. Melt together 1 oz unsweetened chocolate together with 1 T. butter and mix well. Spread over chilled firm frosting, spreading to edges. Refrigerate. Cut into thin bars.
NOTE: I usually double the recipe and make these in a 9" x 13" pan.

SUGAR 'N SPICE NUTS

3 C. lightly salted mixed nuts
1 egg white
1 T. orange juice
2/3 C. sugar

1 T. grated orange peel
1 tsp. ground cinnamon
1/2 tsp. ground ginger
1/2 tsp. ground allspice

Place nuts in a large bowl. Beat egg whites and orange juice in a small bowl with a fork, until foamy. Add sugar, orange peel, cinnamon, ginger and allspice. Mix well. Pour over nuts and stir to coat. Spread into a ungreased 10" x 15" pan. Bake at 275° for 45 - 50 minutes (stirring every 15 minutes) or until nuts are crisp and lightly browned. Cool completely. Store in an airtight container.

CARAMELS

8 oz. butter
1 C. sugar
1 C. brown sugar

1 C. Karo Light syrup
1 can sweetened condensed milk

In a heavy sauce pan, bring all ingredients to a rolling boil, stirring constantly. Over low heat, boil until it reaches 240° (approximately 25 minutes). Pour into well buttered 9" x 13" pan. Cool, then cut into squares and wrap in waxed paper.

PEANUT BUTTER FUDGE

18 oz. jar creamy peanut butter
7 oz. jar marshmallow cream
3 C. sugar

3/4 C. evaporated milk
1 C. peanuts, finely chopped
1 tsp. vanilla

Pour peanut butter and marshmallow into large bowl. In a sauce pan bring sugar and milk to a boil for 5 minutes, stirring constantly. Pour hot sugar mix over peanut butter mix, stir till blended. Stir in peanuts and vanilla. Working quickly pour into a lightly greased 9" x 13" pan. Chill 1 hour, then cut into squares.

FUDGE (AS GOOD AS FANNY FARMER)

1 C. whole milk
4 C. sugar
1 tsp. vanilla
8 oz. butter
25 large marshmallows. Cut in quarters

2 oz. unsweetened chocolate
12 oz. semi-sweet chocolate
1.3 oz. milk chocolate, (Hershey's Bar)
1 C. walnuts, chopped

Mix together milk, sugar, vanilla and butter in a sauce pan. Bring to a boil and boil for 2 minutes. Remove pan from heat. Add marshmallows and stir until melted. Add chocolate one kind at a time, stir rapidly until melted. Mix in nuts and pour into a well buttered 9" x 13" pan. Cut into small squares when chilled. Enjoy a rich tasty treat.
NOTE: Best if no substitutions are made.

ENGLISH TOFFEE (HEATH BARS)

1 C. chopped, roasted, unbleached, almonds
1 C. butter
1 C. white sugar, granulated

1/3 C. brown sugar
2 T. water
1/2 tsp. baking soda
3 oz. chocolate chips

Sprinkle half of almonds into a buttered 9" x 13" pan. Melt butter in a heavy sauce pan. Add sugars and water. Bring to a boil, stirring constantly to 300° or hard crack stage. Stir in baking soda, working fast. Pour over almonds in pan. Let cool 5 minutes. Score with butter knife occasionally dipped in cold water. Melt chocolate chips and pour over top. Sprinkle remainder of almonds on top and press lightly. Cool.

TOFFEE

1 C. walnuts, chopped
1/2 C. butter
3/4 C. brown sugar, packed

1/2 C. semi sweet chocolate chips

Spread walnuts into a 8" x 8" buttered pan. Melt butter and sugar in a sauce pan, bring to a boil stirring constantly. Cook till mix darkens (about 7 minutes). Pour over walnuts. Sprinkle chocolate chips over top. Cover with baking sheet to hold heat. Spread chocolate and refrigerate. Break into pieces when cool.

CHOCOLATE BILLIONARES

1 pkg. (14 oz.) caramels
3 T. water
1 1/2 C. pecans, chopped

1 C. crisp rice cereal
3 C. chocolate chips
1 1/2 tsp. butter

Line 2 baking sheets with wax paper, grease the paper. Combine the caramels and water in sauce pan. Cook and stir over low heat till smooth. Stir in pecans and cereal till coated. Drop by teaspoon onto the prepared pans and refrigerate till firm. Melt chips and butter in microwave until smooth. Roll caramel mixture into 1" balls and immediately dip candy into chocolate. Coat completely with chocolate. Using a fork, lift the candy pieces out of the chocolate, tap off excess chocolate, and place back on pans. Refrigerate.

STAINED GLASS (HARD CANDY)

1/2 C. water
2 C. sugar
1/2 C. light corn syrup
8-12 drops oil flavoring
  (cinnamon is very potent)

3-4 drops food coloring
Powdered sugar

Combine water, sugar and corn syrup and bring to 300°, using a candy thermometer. Remove from heat and add food coloring and oil flavoring. Cool slightly. Pour into greased jelly roll pan. Cool. When cool enough to handle cut into bite size pieces. (Or, drop pan on counter when cool to let the candy break into irregular pieces.) Put pieces into bag filled with powdered sugar to coat. Store in covered container.

CREAM CHEESE AFTER DINNER MINTS

1-3 oz. pkg. cream cheese, softened
2 1/2 C. powdered sugar

2-3 drops food coloring
1 tsp. peppermint flavoring
Granulated sugar

Combine cream cheese, flavoring and food coloring. Work in powdered sugar, first with a spoon, then knead with hands. Mix until well blended and of a dough like consistency. Roll into 1/2" balls. Roll into granulated sugar. Press into a candy mold and release immediately. Or, place balls on waxed paper and flatten with a flat bottomed glass. Let mints set to form a crust. Store in a covered container. Yields 40-50 patties.

Don't argue with an idiot;
people watching may not be able to tell the difference.

Miscellaneous

OVEN OMELET

1/4 C. butter or margarine
18 eggs, beaten
1 C. sour cream
1 C. milk
2 tsp. salt

1/4 C. green pepper, chopped
1/4 C. onion, chopped
2 C. cheddar cheese, shredded
2 C. ham, cubed
1 small can mushrooms, sliced

Heat oven to 325°. Melt butter or margarine in a 9" x 13" glass pan and coat the bottom and sides. In a large bowl, mix remaining ingredients together. Pour into prepared pan. Bake for 1 hour 15 minutes. Cut into squares. Serves about 10 to 12.

BREAKFAST CASSEROLE

5 C. cubed bread, buttered
2 C. ham, diced
1 can mushrooms
1 C. cheddar cheese, shredded
3 eggs

1/2 tsp. salt
1/2 tsp. pepper
1/2 tsp. dry mustard
2 C. milk

Spray a 9" x 13" pan with cooking spray. Layer the bread, ham, mushrooms and cheese in pan. Beat the eggs, salt, pepper, mustard and milk together. Pour egg mixture over layers in pan. Refrigerate overnight. Bake at 325° for 1 hour 10 minutes. Serves 10 to 12.

BREAKFAST PIZZA

12 oz. breakfast sausage links
1 C. cheddar cheese, shredded
1 pkg. refrigerated crescent rolls
6 eggs
1 C. shredded potatoes, frozen or refrigerated

1/2 C. milk
1/8 tsp. cayenne pepper
1/4 tsp. basil
1/4 C. Parmesan cheese

Prepare sausage according to package instructions. Slice links into 1/4" thick coins. Separate the crescent rolls and arrange on a 12" deep dish pizza pan with sides. Place points to center and press to cover bottom and sides of pan. Cover with hash browns, sausage coins, and cheddar cheese. Combine eggs, milk and spices. Mix well. Pour over cheese layer and top with Parmesan cheese. Bake 375° for 20 to 25 minutes or until the eggs are set. Serves 6 to 8 generously.

STUFFED FRENCH TOAST

2 Eggs
2 T. milk
1 tsp. sugar
4 Slices of Texas toast

3 oz. cream cheese
Berry syrup (or pie filling)
Whipped cream (optional)

Beat eggs, milk and sugar in a shallow bowl. Preheat griddle to med/high heat. Spray lightly with non-stick spray. Dip Texas toast in egg mixture (quickly) coating both sides, and place on prepared pan. Repeat with remaining pieces. Cook for about 3 minutes or until lightly browned, then flip toast to brown the other side. Meanwhile, cut cream cheese in half so you have two flat, 3 x 3" squares. Flatten on small plate and warm in microwave for about 20 seconds. Don't cook, just warm. When toast is done, remove from heat. Place the cream cheese on one slice of toast and top with the other piece. Lightly press together. Serve with berry syrup, warmed pie filling or mashed, sweetened berries. Top with whipped cream, if desired. Serves 2.

SCALLOPED APPLES

4 medium apples, peeled and sliced thin
4 T. brown sugar

1/2 C. margarine, melted
2 tsp. cinnamon
2 tsp. brandy extract, optional

Lightly spray a 7" x 11" microwavable dish with non stick spray. Mix all ingredients together in a bowl. Pour into prepared dish. Cover and microwave 4 minutes. Stir and microwave another 3 to 5 minutes or until apples are tender. This can be used to top the stuffed french toast, or serve warm with ice cream.

EASY MICROWAVE BAKED APPLES

4 Apples, cored, peeled and sliced

1/4 C. maple syrup
2 T. pecans, chopped

Spray an 8x8" microwave dish with non stick spray. Arrange apples in dish and drizzle with maple syrup. Sprinkle pecans over top. Cover and microwave on high for 3-4 minutes. Serve warm.

FRUIT AND NUT GRANOLA

5 C. quick oats
1 C. shredded coconut
1/2 C. sunflower seeds
1/2 C. sesame seeds
1 C. mixed nuts
1 C. nonfat dry milk
1 C. wheat germ
3 tsp. cinnamon

1 C. margarine or butter
1/2 C. brown sugar
1/2 C. honey
1/4 C. molasses
1 T. vanilla
1 tsp. salt
1-2 C. dried fruit, dates or raisins (or combination)

In a large roasting pan, place oats, coconut, seeds, nuts, dry milk, wheat germ and cinnamon. Mix well. In a sauce pan, combine margarine, brown sugar, honey, molasses, vanilla and salt. Bring to a boil and cook for 1 minute. Pour over oat mixture and stir to coat. Roast in a 250° oven for 2 hours, stirring every 20 minutes. When cool, mix in dried fruit. May also add chocolate chips, if desired. Makes a great snack.

CHERRY FRUIT CAKE

1 1/2 C. flour
1 1/2 C. sugar
1 tsp. baking powder
1 tsp. salt
2-7 oz. pkg. pitted dates
1 lb. dried candied pineapple, diced

2-16 oz. jars marchino cherries
5 1/2 C. pecan halves
6 eggs
1/3 C. dark rum
2 T. Karo syrup

Grease two 9" x 5" x 3" loaf pans (or use 5 mini loaf pans). Line them with aluminum foil, leaving an overhang of about 2". Grease pans again. Preheat oven to 300°. In a large bowl, sift flour, sugar, baking powder, and salt. Add all the fruit and nuts and toss until well coated. In a small bowl, beat the eggs and rum. Pour over the fruit mixture. Using clean hands, mix thoroughly. Divide in two portions and press very firmly into the prepared pans. Bake in preheated oven for 1 3/4 hours or until toothpick inserted in center of loaf comes out clean. Allow to cool for 15 minutes. Remove from pans and take off foil. Add a little rum to Karo syrup to thin. Using a pastry brush, coat the tops of the loaves with mixture while still warm. Cool thoroughly. Wrap in cling wrap and foil. Can be stored in the freezer for up to a year.

FUNNEL CAKE

1 C. + 2 tsp. flour, sifted
1 tsp. baking powder
1/8 tsp. salt
3/4 C. milk

1 egg, beaten
1 tsp. almond extract
1/2 C. powdered sugar
Canola oil

Mix flour, baking powder and salt with a wire whisk or fork. Add egg and extract and mix until well blended. In a 12" skillet heat 3/4" oil to 350°. Make sure the oil is not heated over 350°, and hold the funnel high enough that any splatter that may occur does not cause injury. Pour 1/4 cup batter into funnel (with narrow spout) while holding finger over spout. Over hot oil, let batter run out in a stream while making a spiral. Fry 3 to 5 minutes till golden brown, turning once. Drain well on paper towel. Sprinkle lightly with powdered sugar. Serve warm. Makes 7 servings.

SOPAPILLAS

1 tube refrigerated crescent rolls
   (8)
4 oz. canola oil

1 pt. vanilla ice cream
2 oz. honey
1 tsp. cinnamon

Remove rolls from tube. Spread out and press the perforations together to form 4 rectangles. Put oil in frying pan and fry each rectangle until browned on each side, turning once. Serve on individual plates, topped with ice cream, drizzled with honey and sprinkled with cinnamon. Makes 4 servings.

PUMPKIN PUDDING

1 small pkg. instant vanilla
   pudding mix
1 small pkg. instant butterscotch
   pudding mix
3 C. milk

1 large can pumpkin (not pie
   filling)
1-2 tsp. pumpkin pie spice (to
   taste)

Mix pudding mixes and milk with a wire whisk until thickened. Add pumpkin and spice. Mix until well blended. Chill. Makes 6 servings.

ORANGE DREAMSICLE DESSERT

1 small box orange Jello
1 small box instant vanilla
  pudding
1 can mandarin oranges
8 oz. Cool Whip
4-6 large oranges

In a large bowl, dissolve Jello in 1 cup of boiling water. Put 3-4 ice cubes in a measuring cup and fill to the 1 cup mark. Add to the hot mixture. Stir until the ice cubes are dissolved. Let cool for 5 minutes. Add the pudding mix into the Jello and beat with electric mixer on high speed until fluffy. Let stand for 15 minutes. Drain the mandarin oranges well. Gently fold in the Cool Whip and the oranges. Refrigerate until ready to serve.

NOTE: To make this a WOW dessert, serve the pudding mix in orange shells. Slice a thin layer of orange peeling off the bottom of each orange so it sits level. On the opposite end, cut off about 1/4" of the orange. Using a spoon, carefully scoop out the orange pulp. Fill each orange with pudding mix. If desired, top each filled orange shell with a dollop of whipped cream and some grated orange zest.

You cannot sit on the road to success for if you do, you will get run over.

NOTES

How to Really Love a Child

Be there!
Invent pleasures together.
Say yes as often as possible.
Giggle a lot.
Surprise them.
Hug trees together.
Learn about parenting.
Realize how important it is to be a child.
Go to a movie theater in your pajamas.
Read books out loud with joy.
Let them bang on pots and pans.
Remember how really small they are.
If they're crabby, put them in water.
Say no ONLY when necessary.
Teach feelings.
Heal your own "inside child".
Make loving safe.
Bake a cake and eat it with no hands.
Go find elephants and kiss them.
Plan to build a rocket ship.
Imagine yourself magic.
Listen to them.
Make lots of forts with blankets.
Let your angel fly.
Reveal your own dreams.
Search out the positive.
Keep the gleam in your eye.
Mail letters to God.
Encourage silly.
Plant licorice in your garden.
Open up. Stop yelling.
Express your love. A lot.
Speak kindly.
Paint their tennis shoes.
Handle with caring.

Children are miraculous!

Kids' Kitchen Crafts

Homemade Glitter	2
Silly Putty	2
Bubble Juice	3
Bubble Wands	3
Chocolate Scented Playdough	3
Bread Dough Basket	4
Rock Candy Stir Sticks	5
Birdie "Tweet" Treats	5
Colored Vases	6
Colorful Salt Art Creations	6
Beauty Bath Bars	7
Cinnamon Holiday Ornaments	7
Mini Log Cabin	8
Apple Doll	9
Apple Spice Potpourri	9
Finger Paints	10
Scented Rocks	10
Eggshell Chalk	11
Spray Chalk	11
Artificial Snow	12
Colored Pasta Art	12
Juggling Balls	13
Marbled Paper	13
Homemade Glue	14
Modeling Clay	14
Doggie Biscuits	15
Invisible Writing	16
The Butter Factory	16

Homemade Glitter

Makes ½ cup

½ C. salt **3 drops food coloring**

Preheat oven to 350°. In a small bowl, place salt. Add drops of any color food coloring. Mix lightly until salt is thoroughly colored. Spread salt mixture in a single layer on a baking sheet. Bake in preheated oven for 10 minutes. Remove baking sheet, being careful not to spill the glitter. Let glitter cool completely on baking sheet before transferring to a storage container.

Silly Putty

Makes about 1 cup

½ C. Elmer's white glue **3 drops food coloring**
½ C. liquid starch

Place white glue in a medium shallow dish. Slowly add liquid starch to glue, kneading with your fingers. The more you handle the silly putty, the better it will turn out! If desired, add drops of any color food coloring and continue to knead with your hands until color is fully incorporated.

Chocolate Scented Playdough

Makes about 2 cups

1¼ C. flour
½ C. salt
½ C. cocoa powder
½ T. cream of tartar
½ T. vegetable oil
1 C. boiling water

In a medium saucepan over medium heat, combine flour, cocoa powder, salt and cream of tartar. Add vegetable oil and boiling water and mix well. Cook, stirring frequently, until mixture forms a soft dough. Remove from heat and let cool. When mixture has cooled, continue to knead with your hands. Store mixture in an airtight container. Kids will enjoy creating shapes and characters with this sweet-smelling playdough!

Bubble Juice

Makes about 1½ cups

1 C. water
2 T. light corn syrup
  or 2 tsp. glycerin
4 T. liquid dishwashing soap

In a large shallow dish, combine water, corn syrup and dishwashing soap. Mix thoroughly and use with homemade bubble wands.

Bubble Wands

Form wire clothes hangers or thin pieces of wire into various shapes. Lightly dip the wands into the bubble juice and wave through the air to make big bubbles!

Bread Dough Basket

Makes 1 basket

1½ C. warm water
1 lb. salt

2 lbs. flour
Clear gloss varnish

Preheat oven to 250°. In a large bowl, combine warm water and salt. Let mixture cool and slowly add flour, mixing constantly, until a firm dough forms. Knead dough with hands until mixture has an elastic feel. Cover mixture with a damp cloth and let sit for 30 minutes. Measure the diameter of an ovenproof baking dish. Roll out dough to desired thickness and cut dough into strips that are about 1″ longer than the diameter of the dish. Lay the strips horizontally across the dish from the top of one side, down over the base of the dish and up the opposite side of the dish. Continue laying the strips, leaving a gap of about 1″ between each strip. When the baking dish has been covered in one direction, begin weaving strips in the opposite direction, alternating going over one strip and under the next. Continue this weaving method by placing the next strip so it goes under and over the opposite strips. Trim any uneven edges with a knife. Roll remaining dough into thin 5″ long strips. Lay the strips end-to-end along the rim of the dish until rim is completely covered. Run your fingers over the dough to create a smooth finish around the rim. To give the rim of the basket a ribbed effect, make small cuts with a knife around the rim. Bake in oven for 1½ to 2 hours, until dough is golden brown and hard to the touch. Remove from oven and let cool completely before removing bread basket from baking dish. Using a medium brush, paint basket with clear gloss varnish. Let varnish dry and apply another coat. When varnish has dried completely, use basket to hold fresh fruits or bread rolls. Do not eat the basket!

Rock Candy Stir Sticks

Makes 5 to 6 sticks

2 C. water
5 C. sugar
Drops of food coloring
Plastic container lid

Wooden coffee stir sticks, bamboo skewers or popsicle sticks

In a large saucepan over medium high heat, place water. Bring to a boil and stir in sugar. Continue to boil until mixture reaches 260°. Remove from heat and let mixture cool for 5 minutes. Pour sugar mixture into glass jar and add drops of food coloring. Mix lightly. Punch stir sticks through the plastic container lid. Set lid over glass jar so the sticks hang down into the sugar mixture but do not touch the bottom of the jar. Set the mixture aside for 7 days. After 7 days, carefully lift the lid out of the jar and you will find magical rock candy stir sticks. Give the sticks as gifts for grown-ups to stir in their coffee or tea.

Birdie "Tweet" Treats

Makes 3 wreaths

8 T. water, divided
1-¼ oz. pkg. unflavored gelatin
2 C. wild birdseed

3-4″ mini bundt or fluted pans
3-12″ pieces colorful ribbon

In a medium saucepan over medium heat, bring 6 tablespoons water to a boil. In a medium bowl, combine unflavored gelatin and remaining 2 tablespoons water. Let mixture sit for 1 minute and then add boiling water. Stir for 2 to 3 minutes, until gelatin is completely dissolved. Stir wild birdseed into gelatin mixture, stirring well. Let mixture sit for a few minutes and stir again. Repeat this process twice, allowing the bird seed to absorb the liquid. Divide the mixture evenly into the miniature bundt pans. Place the filled pans in the refrigerator for 3 hours. Remove the wreaths from the molds by inverting and carefully tapping on the bottom of each pan. Let wreaths dry overnight. Thread one piece of ribbon through each wreath and tie closed. Hang the treats outside for birds to enjoy!

Colorful Salt Art Creations

Makes about 2 creations

1 C. table salt
Various pieces of colored chalk
2 empty baby food jars
Toothpicks

Divide the salt into separate small ziplock bags. Place one piece of colored chalk in each bag with the salt. Close the bags and rub the salt and chalk together by hand until the salt is completely colored. Remove leftover pieces of chalk from the bags. Pour salt in any pattern or order, alternating colors, into the baby food jars. Fill jars completely full so the salt will not shift. If desired, create patterns along the inside of the jar by sticking the toothpick into the layers of colored salt. Put a thin line of hot glue along inside of jars and screw lids tightly onto jars. These salt art creations make great gifts or paperweights!

Colored Vases

Makes 2 vases

¼ C. tacky glue
1 tsp. water
1 paintbrush
2 empty bottles, washed
Colored salt (from recipe above)

Use the colored salt from the above recipe to make beautiful vases! In a plastic cup, combine tacky glue and water. Mix well. Using a paintbrush, apply a thin coat of the glue mixture to the outside of the clean bottles. Pour your colored salt into a cup, using a separate cup for each color. Using one hand, hold one bottle by the tip over a piece of newspaper. While turning the bottle, sprinkle some of the colored sand over the bottle so the salt will attach to the sticky surface. When the bottle is satisfactorily covered with sand, set the bottle aside for 1 day so the glue can dry. Repeat with remaining bottle. Carefully fill the bottles half way with water and display flowers in your homemade vases!

Cinnamon Holiday Ornaments

Makes 12 ornaments

½ C. cinnamon
1 C. applesauce
1 T. nutmeg

1 T. ground cloves
1 T. white glue
Ribbon

In a medium bowl, combine cinnamon, applesauce, nutmeg, ground cloves and glue. Mix well, until a stiff dough forms. Roll out dough to ¼" thickness. Using cookie cutters, cut dough into various shapes. Using the end of a straw, poke a hole into one side of each ornament for the ribbon to go through. Carefully place cut out shapes on a wire rack. Let ornaments air dry for 5 to 7 days, turning occasionally. When ornaments are completely hardened, thread a piece of ribbon through the hole in each ornament and tie a loop so the ornaments can hang. You'll love the smell of these ornaments when placed throughout your home!

Beauty Bath Bar

Makes 1 bar

1 bar soap
Acrylic paints

Paint brushes
2 oz. canning wax

Paint a design over one side of the bar of soap, using the acrylic paints and paint brushes. Meanwhile, in a double boiler over medium high heat, place canning wax. When wax is completely melted, use a disposable brush to paint a layer of clear wax over the painted design on the bar of soap. Set the bar of soap aside until the wax dries. The protective layer of wax will allow the soap to be used while the painted design remains on the bar!

Mini Log Cabin

Makes 1 cabin

- 1 empty ½ pint milk carton
- 1 C. creamy peanut butter
- 50 pretzel sticks
- 1 graham cracker half
- 2 square pretzels or cereal squares
- 12 thin wheat crackers
- 1 pretzel nugget for chimney

Rinse milk carton completely and staple top closed, trimming the top so carton resembles a house shape. Cover sides and top (roof) of carton with creamy peanut butter. Cut pretzel sticks into desired length and cover sides of carton with pretzels, to resemble logs. Use the graham cracker half as a door and the square pretzels or cereal squares for windows. Press the pretzels, cereal and graham crackers into the peanut butter to secure to the carton. Use the thin wheat crackers as overlapping shingles for the roof. Using additional peanut butter, attach the pretzel nugget to the roof as a chimney. Continue to decorate as desired.

Apple Spice Potpourri

Makes about 1½ cups

½ C. chopped dried apple slices
½ C. dried whole cranberries
4 cinnamon sticks

1 whole nutmeg, broken into pieces
2 T. whole cloves
2 T. whole allspice

Place dried apples and cranberries on a baking sheet and set aside to air dry for several days. In a large bowl, combine dried apples, dried cranberries, cinnamon sticks, nutmeg pieces, whole cloves and whole allspice. Mix ingredients together by hand. To simmer the potpourri, in a small saucepan, combine ½ cup of the potpourri mixture and 2 cups water. Place the saucepan over low heat and let simmer for several hours. If mixture begins to dry out, add more water as needed. Simmering potpourri will fill your entire house with a pleasing fragrance!

Apple Doll

Makes 1 doll

1 large Red Delicious apple
Carving knife and potato peeler
Colored markers, optional

1 plastic bottle
Hot glue gun and glue
Various pieces of fabric

Peel and core the apple. With the help of an adult, carefully carve a face shape into the apple, hollowing out deep-set eyes and a deep slit for the mouth. If desired, add extra features like ears or a nose. Set the apple aside for several days, until the apple has shrunk to about ⅔ its original size. When the apple face is completely dried out, go over the eyes and other features with markers, if desired. Cut the top part off of the plastic bottle and apply a line of hot glue. Attach the apple head to the bottle and hold in place until hot glue has dried. Decorate the doll by wrapping fabric around the bottle to make clothes. Enjoy playing with your new doll, but remember that this doll is not for eating!

Finger Paints

Makes about 5 cups

2 C. flour
2 tsp. salt
3 C. cold water
2 C. hot water
Drops of food coloring

In a medium saucepan over medium heat, combine flour and salt. Add cold water and, using a whisk or hand mixer, beat mixture until smooth. Add hot water and bring mixture to a boil, stirring until paint is glossy. Remove from heat and add drops of desired color food coloring. Stir until mixture is completely colored, adding more drops of food coloring if needed. Let paint cool completely before using finger paints in various art projects!

Scented Rocks

Makes about 6 rocks

½ C. wholemeal flour
½ C. salt
¼ tsp. essential oil, any kind
⅔ C. boiling water
Drops of food coloring

In a small bowl, combine flour, salt and essential oil. Mix well and add boiling water. Add drops of any color food coloring and mix well. When mixture has cooled enough to handle, roll mixture into 2″ to 3″ balls. Shape balls into assorted rock shapes. Place "rocks" on a cooling rack in a warm, dry area. After several days, the rocks will be hard. These scented rocks will give a nice fragrance when placed in various dishes around your home.

Eggshell Chalk

Makes 1 chalk stick

4 to 5 egg shells
1 tsp. flour
1 tsp. very hot water
Drops of food coloring, optional

Wash and dry egg shells completely. Place clean and dry egg shells in a small bowl and grind into a fine dust. When egg shells are almost completely ground, discard any larger pieces. In a separate bowl, place flour and hot water. Mix well and add 1 tablespoon of the egg shell powder, stirring until a paste forms. If desired, add drops of any color food coloring and continue to mix. Remove mixture from bowl and shape into a log or chalk stick form. Wrap mixture tightly with a strip of paper towel. Set aside chalk piece and let dry for about 3 days, until hardened. Carefully unwrap paper towel to reveal your homemade chalk. This chalk is for use on sidewalks only!

Spray Chalk

Makes about 1 cup

4 T. cornstarch
1 C. warm water
Drops of food coloring

In a medium bowl, combine cornstarch and warm water, stirring until mixture is smooth. Add drops of any color food coloring and mix well. Pour mixture into a small plastic bottle mister. Shake bottle before using to break up clogs. Use spray chalk to decorate sidewalks or snow. Or use it to create colorful sand sculptures at the beach!

Colored Pasta Art

Makes 2 cups colored pasta

¼ C. rubbing alcohol
1 T. food coloring

2 C. dry pasta, any kind*

In a 1-quart ziplock bag, place rubbing alcohol and food coloring. Securely close bag and shake until well combined. Open bag and add dry pasta. Close bag again and turn in hands to coat pasta with the coloring. Lay bag on a flat surface and let sit for 1 hour. Turn bag over and let sit for an additional 30 minutes. Carefully pour liquid from bag and pour remaining pasta into a large paper bag to dry. Use dried colored pasta to make pictures, sculptures, jewelry or other art projects.

Use various pasta shapes, such as: rigatoni, macaroni, wagon wheel, spiral or bow tie.

Artificial Snow

Makes 1 cup

½ C. sugar
½ C. talcum powder

½ C. white glue
½ C. water

In a medium bowl, combine sugar and talcum powder and set aside. In a separate bowl, combine glue and water. Spread glue mixture over surface that you want to decorate with snow. Sprinkle the sugar mixture over the glue and enjoy the look of sparkling white snow!

Marbled Paper

10 C. cold water
2 or 3 different colors of oil paint

Turpentine
Brown paper bags

In a shallow pan, place cold water. Add one color of the oil paint and a little turpentine until mixture reaches the consistency of thick cream. Drop a few drops of a different colored oil paint into the pan. If the paint drops sink, the mixture is too thick and you should add a little more turpentine. If the paint drops spread, the mixture is too thin and you should add a little more oil paint. When the mixture is the correct consistency, drop large spots of oil paint, one at a time, into the mixture. Using a spoon, stick or comb, swirl the paint into desired marbled patterns. Cut the brown paper bags into pieces that are slightly smaller than the shallow pan. Holding opposite corners of the paper, slowly lower the paper into the mixture in pan until one side of the paper has touched the solution. Carefully lift the paper out of the solution and place, marbled side up, on a stack of newspapers or drying rack. If desired, hang the papers on a clothes line to dry. Use this marbled paper for various art crafts or as stationery.

Juggling Balls

Makes 1 balls

3 plastic baggies
4½ C. dried beans, divided

6 balloons

Fill each plastic baggie with 1½ cups dried beans. Secure baggies with twist ties. Cut the top off of each balloon (the part that you blow into). Stretch one balloon over a filled plastic bag, being sure to cover the twist tie. Stretch another balloon over the baggie to conceal the hole, making sure the plastic bag is completely covered.

Homemade Glue

Makes about 6 cups

1 qt. skim milk
1 T. white vinegar
¾ T. baking soda
10 oz. water

In a double boiler over low heat, place milk and vinegar. Cook, stirring occasionally, until curds begin to form. Remove from heat and pour mixture through a strainer, discarding any remaining liquid. Slowly wash curds under running water until the smell of vinegar has disappeared. Place the curds in a clean, medium bowl. In a separate bowl, combine baking soda and water, stirring until baking soda is completely dissolved. Pour mixture over curds in bowl and stir until a white paste forms. Use glue for craft projects and store in airtight containers.

Modeling Clay

Makes 1½ cups

1 C. baking soda
½ C. cornstarch
¾ C. water
Drops of food coloring

In a medium saucepan over low heat, combine baking soda and cornstarch. Mix well and add water. Continue to heat for 7 to 10 minutes, stirring frequently, until mixture is the consistency of mashed potatoes. Continue to stir, as mixture will thicken very quickly. Cover a flat surface with additional cornstarch. Spread mixture over cornstarch and knead by hand until mixture turns into a workable clay. Divide clay into several sections. Make a hole in the center of each section and add a few drops of food coloring to the hole in each section. If desired, use a different color for each section. Knead the sections by hand until the color has distributed throughout. Use modeling clay to make fun sculptures and creations. For a permanent sculpture, let the modeled clay air dry overnight. Place leftover clay in a ziplock bag and refrigerate. Use leftover clay within 3 days.

Doggie Biscuits

Makes about 2 dozen

¼ C. hot water
1 tsp. sugar
1 pkg. active dry yeast
8 chicken bouillon cubes

1½ C. tomato juice
2 C. flour, divided
2 C. wheat germ
1½ C. whole wheat flour

Preheat oven to 300°. In a large bowl, place hot water. Add sugar and yeast and let stand for about 5 minutes. Crush chicken bouillon cubes with a fork and stir crushed bouillon into yeast mixture. Add tomato juice, 1 cup flour and wheat germ and stir until a smooth batter forms. Add remaining 1 cup flour and whole wheat flour and stir until dough is stiff and very dry. Continue to mix by hand. Turn half of the dough out onto a lightly floured flat surface. Using a rolling pin, roll dough to about ¼" thickness. If dough is too sticky, add additional flour. Using cookie cutters or a knife, cut biscuits into desired shape. Repeat with remaining dough. Place biscuits on a baking sheet and bake in oven for 1 hour. Turn off oven and let biscuits dry and harden in oven for about 4 hours. Remove cooled biscuits from oven and give them as a treat to your favorite dog!

Invisible Writing

Makes about 6 cups

1 small paint brush
1/2 C. lemon juice
White paper

1 medium paint brush
1 C. grape juice

Write a secret message on a piece of paper that only your friends can see! Dip the small paint brush in lemon juice and write your message on the white paper. Your friend can reveal the message by dipping the medium paint brush in grape juice and "painting" over the entire piece of paper. Your secret message will show through!

The Butter Factory

Makes 1½ cups

1 pint heavy whipping cream
Small plastic container with lid

Yellow food coloring, optional

Pour the heavy whipping cream into the plastic container. Securely fasten the lid to the container. Take turns shaking the container with cream vigorously. Continue shaking for 15 to 30 minutes, until the cream has separated into buttermilk and solid butter. Open the container and discard the buttermilk. If desired, stir in a few drops of yellow food coloring until butter reaches desired shade. Use butter for normal purposes. Store in an airtight container in refrigerator.

Cooking & Nutritional Tips

Common Kitchen Pans	2
Equivalents for Cooking Ingredients	3
Substitutions	4
Troubleshooting Baking Failures	6
Uses For Spices & Seasonings	7
Food Storage	8
Measurements/Equivalents	10
USDA Food Guide	11
Calorie Requirements Chart	12
How Much is One Serving?	12
Table of Nutrients	13
Sources for Common Nutrients	13
Healthy Choices	14
Sources of Saturated Fat	14
Physical Activity Recommendations	15
Calories Expended in Physical Activities	16

Common Kitchen Pans

When a recipe calls for...

4 cup baking dish:
- 9 inch pie plate
- 8 x 1¼" layer cake pan
- 7⅜ x 3⅝ x 2¼" loaf pan

6 cup baking dish:
- 8 or 9 x 1½" layer-cake pan
- 10" pie plate
- 8½ x 3⅝ x 2⅝" loaf pan

8 cup baking dish:
- 8 x 8 x 2" square pan
- 11 x 7 x 1½" baking pan
- 9 x 5 x 3" loaf pan

10 cup baking dish:
- 9 x 9 x 2" square pan
- 11¾ x 7½ x 1¾" baking pan
- 15 x 10 x 1" jellyroll pan

12 cup baking dish or over:
- 12⅓ x 8½ x 2" glass baking pan *(12 cups)*
- 13 x 9 x 2" metal baking pan *(15 cups)*
- 14 x 10½ x 2½" roasting pan *(19 cups)*

Total Volume of Various Special Baking Pans...

Tube Pans:
- 7½ x 3" "Bundt" tube *(6 cups)*
- 9 x 3½" fancy tube or "Bundt" pan *(9 cups)*
- 9 x 3½" angel cake pan *(12 cups)*
- 10 x 3¾" "Bundt" or "Crownburst" pan *(12 cups)*
- 9 x 3½" fancy tube *(12 cups)*
- 10 x 4" fancy tube mold (kugelhupf) *(16 cups)*
- 10 x 4" angel cake pan *(18 cups)*

Spring Form Pans:
- 8 x 3" pan *(12 cups)*
- 9 x 3" pan *(16 cups)*

Ring Mold:
- 8½ x 2¼" mold *(4½ cups)*
- 9¼ x 2¾" mold *(8 cups)*

Charlotte Mold:
- 6 x 4¼" mold *(7½ cups)*

Brioche Pan:
- 9½ x 3¼" pan *(8 cups)*

Loaf Pan

Spring Form Pan

Layer-Cake Pan

Square Pan

Ring Mold

Brioche Pan

Charlotte Mold

Angel Cake Pan

Fancy Tube Mold (kugelhupf)

Bundt Pan

Equivalents for Cooking Ingredients

Apples (1 lb.)	3 or 4 medium
Bananas (1 lb.)	3 or 4 medium
Beans, dried (1 lb.)	5 to 6 cups cooked
Berries (1 quart)	3½ cups
Bread (1 slice)	½ cup crumbs
Cheese, grated (¼ lb.)	1 cup
Chocolate, 1 square (1 oz.)	1 T. melted
Cream (½ pint)	1 cup
Cream, heavy (1 cup)	2 cups whipped
Flour, all-purpose (1 lb.)	4 cups sifted
Gelatin (1 envelope)	1 T.
Herbs, dried (1 tsp.)	1 T. fresh
Lemon (2 to 3 T. juice)	1½ tsp. grated rind
Macaroni (1 cup dry)	2¼ cups cooked
Meat, diced (1 lb.)	2 cups
Mushrooms (1 lb.)	5 to 6 cups sliced
Nuts, shelled (¼ lb.)	1 cup chopped
Onion (1 medium)	½ cup chopped
Orange (6 to 8 T. juice)	⅓ to ½ cup pulp
Potatoes (3 medium)	1¾ to 2 cups mashed
Rice (1 cup uncooked)	3 cups cooked
Spaghetti (½ lb.)	3½ to 4 cups cooked
Sugar, confectioners (1 lb.)	4½ cups unsifted
Sugar, granulated (1 lb.)	2 cups
Tomatoes (1 lb.)	3 or 4 medium
Walnuts in shell (1 lb.)	1¾ cups chopped

Substitutions

For:	You Can Use:
1 T. cornstarch	2 T. flour **OR** 1½ T. quick cooking tapioca
1 C. cake flour	1 C. less 2 T. all-purpose flour
1 C. all-purpose flour	1 C. plus 2 T. cake flour
1 square chocolate	3 T. cocoa and 1 T. shortening
1 C. melted shortening	1 C. salad oil (may not be substituted for solid shortening)
1 C. milk	½ C. evaporated milk and ½ C. water
1 C. sour milk or buttermilk	1 T. lemon juice or vinegar and enough sweet milk to measure 1 C.
1 C. heavy cream	⅔ C. milk and ⅓ C. butter
1 C. heavy cream, whipped	⅔ C. well-chilled evaporated milk, whipped
Sweetened condensed milk	No substitution
1 egg	2 T. dried whole egg and 2 T. water
1 tsp. baking powder	¼ tsp. baking soda and 1 tsp. cream of tartar **OR** ¼ tsp. baking soda and ½ C. sour milk, buttermilk or molasses; reduce other liquid ½ C.
1 C. sugar	1 C. honey; reduce other liquid ¼ C.; reduce baking temperature 25°
1 C. miniature marshmallows	About 10 large marshmallows, cut up
1 medium onion (2½" dia.)	2 T. instant minced onion **OR** 1 tsp. onion powder **OR** 2 tsp. onion salt; reduce salt 1 tsp.
1 garlic clove	⅛ tsp. garlic powder **OR** ¼ tsp. garlic salt; reduce salt ⅛ tsp.
1 T. fresh herbs	1 tsp. dried herbs **OR** ¼ tsp. powdered herbs **OR** ½ tsp. herb salt; reduce salt ¼ tsp.
Bread crumbs	Use crushed corn or wheat flakes, or other dry cereal. Or use potato flakes.
Butter	Use 7/8 cup of solid shortening plus 1/2 teaspoon of salt.

Substitutions

For:	You Can Use:
Fresh milk	To substitute 1 cup of fresh milk, use ½ cup each of evaporated milk and water. For 1 cup of whole milk, prepare 1 liquid cup of nonfat dry milk and 2½ teaspoons butter or margarine.
Sugar	Use brown sugar, although it will result in a slight molasses flavor.
Superfine sugar	Process regular granulated sugar in your blender.
Red and green sweet pepper	Use canned pimientos.
Vanilla extract	Use grated lemon or orange rind for flavoring instead. Or try a little cinnamon or nutmeg.
Flour	Substitute 1 tablespoon cornstarch for 2 tablespoons of flour. Or try using instant potatoes or cornmeal.
Buttermilk	Use 1 tablespoon of lemon juice or vinegar and enough fresh milk to make 1 cup. Let it stand 5 minutes before using.
Ketchup	Use a cup of tomato sauce added to 1¼ cups of brown sugar, 2 tablespoons of vinegar, ¼ teaspoon of cinnamon and a dash of ground cloves and allspice.
Unsweetened chocolate	Use 1 tablespoon of shortening plus 3 tablespoons of unsweetened chocolate to equal 1 square of unsweetened chocolate.
Corn syrup	Use ¼ cup of water or other type of liquid called for in the recipe, plus 1 cup of sugar.
Eggs	Add 3 or 4 extra tablespoons of liquid called for in the recipe. Or, when you're 1 egg shy for a recipe that calls for many, substitute 1 teaspoon of cornstarch.
Cake flour	Use ⅞ cup of all-purpose flour for each cup of cake flour called for in a recipe.
Fresh herbs and spices	Use ⅓ the amount of dried herbs or spices. Dried herbs are more concentrated.
Honey	To substitute 1 cup of honey, use 1¼ cups of sugar and ¼ cup of water or other liquid called for in the recipe.

Troubleshooting Baking Failures

Biscuits

1. Rough biscuits caused from insufficient mixing.
2. Dry biscuits caused from baking in too slow an oven and handling too much.
3. Uneven browning caused from cooking in dark surface pan (use a cookie sheet or shallow bright finish pan), too high a temperature and rolling the dough too thin.

Muffins

1. Coarse texture caused from insufficient stirring and cooking at too low a temperature.
2. Tunnels in muffins, peaks in center and soggy texture are caused from overmixing.
3. For a nice muffin, mix well but light and bake at correct temperature.

Cakes

1. Cracks and uneven surface may be caused by too much flour, too hot an oven and sometimes from cold oven start.
2. Cake is dry may be caused by too much flour, too little shortening, too much baking powder or cooking at too low a temperature.
3. A heavy cake means too much sugar has been used or baked too short a period.
4. A sticky crust is caused by too much sugar.
5. Coarse grained cake may be caused by too little mixing, too much fat, too much baking powder, using fat too soft, and baking at too low a temperature.
6. Cakes fall may be caused by using insufficient flour, under baking, too much sugar, too much fat or not enough baking powder.
7. Uneven browning may be caused from cooking cakes at too high a temperature, crowding the shelf (allow at least 2" around pans) or using dark pans (use bright finish, smooth bottomed pans).
8. Cake has uneven color is caused from not mixing well. Mix thoroughly, but do not over mix.

Pies

1. Pastry crumbles caused by overmixing flour and fat.
2. Pastry is tough caused by using too much water and over mixing dough.
3. Pies can burn -for fruit or custard pies use a Pyrex pie pan or enamel pan and bake at 400° to 425° constant temperature.

Breads (Yeast)

1. Yeast bread is porous -this is caused by over-rising or cooking at too low a temperature.
2. Crust is dark and blisters -this is caused by over-rising, the bread will blister just under the crust.
3. Bread does not rise -this is caused from over-kneading or from using old yeast.
4. Bread is streaked -this is caused from underkneading and not kneading evenly.
5. Bread baked uneven -caused by using old dark pans, too much dough in pan, crowding the oven shelf or cooking at too high temperature.

Uses for Spices & Seasonings

All-Spice	Cakes, cookies, pies, breads, puddings, fruit preserves, pickles, relishes, yellow vegetables
Basil	Tomatoes, tomato sauce, barbecue sauce, salads
Celery Seed	Meat loaf; beef, lamb and vegetable stews; bean salad
Cloves	Ham, beets, pickling, beef marinades, hot spiced beverages, cakes, pies, puddings
Chili Powder	Vegetable and beef chili, cocktail and barbecue sauces, egg dishes, meatballs, meat loaf
Thyme	Chowder, seafood, stuffing, poultry, meat, vegetables
Dill	Salads and salad dressings, sour cream or mayonnaise dips, eggs, cucumbers, tomatoes, carrots, fish, cheese dishes
Garlic	Nearly all types of meat, fish, poultry, vegetables, sauces, stews, soups, salads and salad dressings
Rosemary	Lamb, poultry stuffing, beef and pork roasts, tomato sauce, salads, seafood, turnips, potatoes, cauliflower
Sage	Veal, sausage, poultry, stuffings, cheese spreads, soups
Tarragon	Salad dressings, sauces, egg dishes, stews, poultry, seafood
Cinnamon	Cakes, cookies, pies, puddings, coffee, dessert topping, yellow vegetables, hot spiced beverages

Food Storage

Baking Powder: Store the airtight tins in a cool, dry place and replace every 6 months.

Baking Soda: Store in an airtight container in a cool, dry place for about 6 months.

Beans: Once a package is opened, dry beans should not be refrigerated but stored in airtight containers in a cold, dry place. They will keep for about 1 year.

Bread: A rib of celery in your bread bag will keep the bread fresh for a longer time.

Brown Sugar: Wrap in a plastic bag and store in a tightly covered container for up to 4 months.

Cakes: Putting half an apple in the cake box will keep cake moist.

Celery and lettuce: Store in refrigerator in paper bags instead of plastic. Leave the outside leaves and stalks on until ready to use.

Cheese: Wrap cheese in a vinegar-dampened cloth to keep it from drying out.

Chocolate: Store chocolate for no longer than 1 year. It should be kept in a cool, dry place with a temperature range of 60°F to 75°F. If the storage temperature exceeds 75°F, some of the cocoa butter may separate and rise to the surface, causing a whitish color to the chocolate called "bloom".

Cocoa: Store cocoa in a glass jar in a dry and cool place.

Cookies: Place crushed tissue paper on the bottom of your cookie jar.

Cottage Cheese: Store carton upside-down. It will keep twice as long.

Dried Fruit: Store unopened packages of dried fruit in a cool, dry place or in the refrigerator. Store opened packages in an airtight container in the refrigerator or freezer for 6 to 8 months.

Flour: Store flour in a clean, tightly covered container for up to 1 year at room temperature.

Garlic: Garlic should be stored in a dry, airy place away from light. Garlic cloves can be kept in the freezer. When ready to use, peel and chop before thawing. Or, garlic cloves will never dry out if you store them in a bottle of cooking oil. After the garlic is used up, you can use the garlic flavored oil for salad dressing.

Granulated Sugar: Store sugar in a tightly covered container for up to 2 years.

Honey: Put honey in small plastic freezer containers to prevent sugaring. It also thaws out in a short time.

Ice Cream: Ice cream that has been opened and returned to the freezer sometimes forms a waxlike film on the top. To prevent this, after part of the ice cream has been removed press a piece of waxed paper against the surface and reseal the carton.

Lemons: Store whole lemons in a tightly sealed jar of water in the refrigerator. They will yield much more juice than when first purchased.

Limes: Store limes, wrapped in tissue paper, on lower shelf of the refrigerator.

Marshmallows: They will not dry out if stored in the freezer. Simply cut with scissors when ready to use.

Nuts: For optimum freshness and shelf life, nuts should be stored, preferably unshelled, in a tightly covered container in the refrigerator or freezer and shelled as needed. (The shell and the cool temperature keep the nut from turning rancid.)

Olive Oil: You can lengthen the life of olive oil by adding a cube of sugar to the bottle.

Food Storage

Onions: Wrap individually in foil to keep them from becoming soft or sprouting. Once an onion has been cut in half, rub the leftover side with butter and it will keep fresh longer.

Parsley: Keep fresh and crisp by storing in a wide-mouth jar with a tight lid. Parsley may also be frozen.

Popcorn: It should always be kept in the freezer. Not only will it stay fresh, but freezing helps eliminate "old-maids".

Potatoes: Potatoes, as well as other root vegetables, keep well in a dark, cool place, preferably a cellar. Store them in a dark brown paper bag.

Shredded Coconut: Store in a cool, dry place in an airtight container. Do not store in the refrigerator.

Smoked Meats: Wrap ham or bacon in a vinegar-soaked cloth, then in waxed paper to preserve freshness.

Soda Crackers: Wrap tightly and store in the refrigerator.

Strawberries: Keep in a colander in the refrigerator. Wash just before serving.

Vegetables with tops: Remove the tops on carrots, beets, etc. before storing.

Yeast: Store in the freezer or refrigerator in a closed plastic bag.

MEAT

Beef

Roasts	3 to 5 days
Steaks	3 to 5 days
Ground beef, stew meat	2 days

Pork

Roasts	3 to 5 days
Hams, picnics, whole	7 days
Bacon	7 to 14 days
Chops, spareribs	2 to 3 days
Pork sausage	1 to 2 days

Veal

Roasts	3 to 5 days
Chops	4 days

Lamb

Roasts	3 to 5 days
Chops	3 to 5 days
Ground lamb	2 days

Poultry

Chickens, whole	1 to 2 days
Chickens, cut up	2 days
Turkeys, whole	1 to 2 days

Cooked meats

Leftover cooked meats	4 days
Cooked poultry	2 days
Hams, picnics	7 days
Frankfurters	4 to 5 days
Sliced luncheon meats	3 days
Unsliced bologna	4 to 6 days

Measurements/Equivalents

Metric Volume Measurements

Measure	*Equivalent*
1 cubic centimeter	0.061 cubic inch
1 cubic inch	16.39 cubic centimeters
1 cubic decimeter	0.0353 cubic foot
1 cubic foot	28.317 cubic decimeters
1 cubic yard	0.7646 cubic meter
1 cubic meter	0.2759 cord
1 cord	3.625 steres
1 liter	0.908 qt. dry (1.0567 qts. liquid)
1 quart dry	1.101 liters
1 quart liquid	0.9463 liter
1 dekaliter	2.6417 gallons (1.135 pecks)
1 gallon	0.3785 dekaliter
1 peck	0.881 dekaliter
1 hektoliter	2.8378 bushels
1 bushel	0.3524 hektoliter

Simplified Measurements

1 tablespoon	3 teaspoons
2 tablespoons	1 ounce
1 jigger	1½ ounces
¼ cup	4 tablespoons
⅓ cup	5 tablespoons plus 1 teaspoon
½ cup	8 tablespoons
1 cup	16 tablespoons
1 pint	2 cups
1 quart	4 cups
1 gallon	4 quarts
1 liter	4 cups plus 3 tablespoons
1 ounce (dry)	2 tablespoons
1 pound	16 ounces

USDA Food Guide

Amounts in each food group are recommended for most adults at a daily 2,000 calorie level diet.

Food Group	USDA Daily Recommendation	Equivalent Amounts
Fruits	2 cups (4 servings)	½ cup is equivalent to: • ½ cup fresh, frozen or canned fruit • 1 medium fruit • ¼ cup dried fruit • ½ cup fruit juice
Vegetables	2½ cups (5 servings)	½ cup is equivalent to: • ½ cup raw or cooked vegetables • 1 cup raw leafy vegetables • ½ cup vegetable juice
Grains	6 ounces	1 ounce is equivalent to: • 1 slice bread • 1 cup dry cereal • ½ cup cooked rice, pasta or cereal
Meats & Beans	5½ ounces	1 ounce is equivalent to: • 1 ounce cooked lean meat, poultry or fish • 1 egg • ¼ cup cooked dry beans or tofu • 1 tablespoon peanut butter
Milk	3 cups	1 cup is equivalent to: • 1 cup low-fat or fat-free milk or yogurt • 1½ ounces low-fat or fat-free natural cheese • 2 ounces low-fat or fat-free processed cheese
Oils	24 grams (6 teaspoons)	1 teaspoon is equivalent to: • 1 teaspoon soft margarine • 1 tablespoon low-fat mayonnaise • 2 tablespoons light salad dressing • 1 teaspoon vegetable oil
Discretionary	267 calories (2⅔ T. sugars)	1 tablespoon is equivalent to: • 1 tablespoon jelly or jam • ½ ounce jelly beans • 8 ounces lemonade

The 2,000 calorie USDA Food Guide is appropriate for many sedentary males 51 to 70 years of age, sedentary females 19 to 30 years of age and for some other gender or age groups who are more physically active. The oils listed in this table are not considered to be part of discretionary calories because they are a major source of Vitamin E and polyunsaturated fatty acids, including the essential fatty acids, in the food pattern. In contrast, solid fats (i.e., saturated and trans fats) are listed separately as a source of discretionary calories.

Source: USDA Dietary Guidelines for Americans 2005, Table 1.

Calorie Requirements Chart

Estimated amounts of calories required to maintain energy balance for certain gender and age groups at three different levels of physical activity. Estimates are rounded to the nearest 200 calories and were determined using the Institute of Medicine equation.

Gender	Age	Sedentary	Activity Level — Moderately Active	Active
Child	2 to 3	1,000	1,000 to 1,400	1,000 to 1,400
Female	4 to 8	1,200	1,400 to 1,600	1,400 to 1,800
	9 to 13	1,600	1,600 to 2,000	1,800 to 2,200
	14 to 18	1,800	2,000	2,400
	19 to 30	2,000	2,000 to 2,200	2,400
	31 to 50	1,800	2,000	2,200
	51+	1,600	1,800	2,000 to 2,200
Male	4 to 8	1,400	1,400 to 1,600	1,600 to 2,000
	9 to 13	1,800	1,800 to 2,200	2,000 to 2,600
	14 to 18	2,200	2,400 to 2,800	2,800 to 3,200
	19 to 30	2,400	2,600 to 2,800	3,000
	31 to 50	2,200	2,400 to 2,600	2,800 to 3,000
	51+	2,000	2,200 to 2,400	2,400 to 2,800

Source: *USDA Dietary Guidelines for Americans 2005, Table 3.*

How Much is One Serving?

Milk & Milk Products	• 1 C. (8 oz.) milk or yogurt • 2 (¾ oz.) slices cheese (⅛″ thick)	• 2 C. cottage cheese • 1½ C. ice cream or frozen yogurt
Meat & Meat Alternatives	• 2 to 3 oz. cooked lean meat, poultry or fish • 2 eggs • 7 oz. tofu	• 1 C. cooked dried beans or peas • 4 T. peanut butter • ½ C. nuts or seeds
Vegetables	• ½ C. cooked vegetables • ½ C. raw chopped vegetables	• 1 C. raw leafy vegetables • ½ to ¾ C. vegetable juice
Fruits	• 1 whole medium fruit (about 1 cup) • ¼ C. dried fruit	• ½ C. canned fruit • ½ to ¾ C. fruit juice
Bread & Cereal	• 1 slice bread • 1 medium muffin • ½ hot dog bun or hamburger bun • ½ bagel or English muffin • 4 small crackers	• 1 tortilla • 1 C. cold cereal • ½ C. cooked cereal • ½ C. rice • ½ C. pasta

Source: *USDA Dietary Guidelines for Americans 2005, Table 3.*

Table of Nutrients

Estimated nutrient intake levels recommended by the USDA at the daily 2,000 calorie level, as well as recommendations by the Institute of Medicine (IOM) for females 19 to 30 years of age.

Nutrient	USDA	IOM for females 19 to 30*
Protein, g	91	RDA: 56
Carbohydrate, g	271	RDA: 130
Total Fat, g	65	–
Saturated Fat, g	17	–
Monounsaturated Fat, g	24	–
Polyunsaturated Fat, g	20	–
Total Dietary Fiber, g	31	AI: 28
Cholesterol, mg	230	ALAP
Potassium, mg	4,044	AI: 4,700
Sodium, mg	1,779	AI: 1,500, UL:<2,300
Calcium, mg	1,316	AI: 1,000
Magnesium, mg	380	RDA: 310
Iron, mg	18	RDA: 18
Phosphorous, mg	1,740	RDA: 700
Zinc, mg	14	RDA: 8
Riboflavin, mg	2.8	RDA: 1.1
Vitamin B6, mg	2.4	RDA: 1.3
Vitamin B12	8.3	RDA: 2.4
Vitamin C	155	RDA: 75
Vitamin E	9.5	RDA: 15
Vitamin A	1,052	RDA: 700

***RDA**= Recommended Daily Allowance, **AI**= Adequate Intake, **AMDR**= Acceptable Macronutrient Distribution Range, **UL**= Upper Limit, **ALAP**= As Low As Possible while consuming a nutritionally adequate diet.

Source: USDA Dietary Guidelines for Americans 2005, Table 2.

Sources for Common Nutrients

Vitamin A
- Bright orange vegetables like carrots, sweet potatoes and pumpkin
- Tomatoes, tomato products and red sweet peppers
- Leafy greens, such as spinach, collards, turnip greens, kale, beet and mustard greens, green leaf lettuce and romaine
- Orange fruits like mango, cantaloupe, apricots and red or pink grapefruit

Vitamin C
- Citrus fruits and juices, kiwi fruit, strawberries, guava, papaya and cantaloupe
- Broccoli, peppers, tomatoes, cabbage (especially Chinese cabbage), brussels sprouts and potatoes
- Leafy greens, such as romaine, turnip greens and spinach

Potassium
- Baked white or sweet potatoes, cooked greens or spinach, orange squash
- Bananas, plantains, many diced fruits, oranges and orange juice, cantaloupe and honeydew melons
- Cooked dry beans
- Soybeans (green and mature)
- Tomato products (sauce, paste or puree)
- Beet greens

Source: USDA Dietary Guidelines for Americans 2005, Table 5.

Healthy Choices

This table shows the differences in saturated fat and calorie content of commonly consumed foods. Comparisons are made between foods in the same food group.

Food Group	Portion	Saturated Fat (g)	Calories
CHEESE			
Regular Cheddar cheese	1 oz.	6.0	114
Low-fat Cheddar cheese	1 oz.	1.2	49
MEATS & POULTRY			
Regular ground beef	3 oz.	6.1	236
Extra lean ground beef	3 oz.	2.6	148
Fried chicken leg	3 oz.	3.3	212
Roasted chicken breast	3 oz.	0.9	140
Fried fish	3 oz.	2.8	195
Baked fish	3 oz.	1.5	129
MILK			
Whole milk	1 C.	4.6	146
Low-fat milk (1%)	1 C.	1.5	102
BREADS			
Croissant	Medium	6.6	231
Oat bran bagel (4″)	Medium	0.2	227
DESSERTS			
Regular ice cream	½ C.	4.9	145
Low-fat frozen yogurt	½ C.	2.0	110
OILS			
Butter	1 tsp.	2.4	34
Soft margarine	1 tsp.	0.7	25

Source: USDA Dietary Guidelines for Americans 2005, Table 9.

Sources of Saturated Fat

This table shows major dietary sources of saturated fats in the U.S. diet, with a mean average daily intake of 25.5 grams. Saturated fats make the body produce more cholesterol, which can raise blood cholesterol levels and lead to cardiovascular disease. Contribution shows percent of total saturated fat consumed.

Food Group	Contribution	Food Group	Contribution
Cheese	13.1	Shortening	4.4
Beef	11.7	Salad Dressing/Mayonnaise	3.7
Milk	7.8	Poultry	3.6
Oils	4.9	Margarine	3.2
Ice Cream/Sherbet/Frozen Yogurt	4.7	Sausage	3.1
Cakes/Cookies/Quick Bread/Donuts	4.7	Potato Chips/Corn Chips/Popcorn	2.9
Butter	4.6	Yeast Bread	2.6
		Eggs	2.3

Source: USDA Dietary Guidelines for Americans 2005, Table 10.

Physical Activity Recommendations

Physical Activity Recommendations Per Age Group

Children & Adolescents
Engage in at least 1 hour of physical activity on most or all days of the week.

Pregnant Women
In the absence of medical or obstetric complications, engage in 30 minutes or more of moderate-intensity physical activity on most or all days of the week. Avoid activities with a high risk of falling or abdominal trauma.

Breastfeeding Women
Be aware that neither acute nor regular exercise will adversely affect the mother's ability to successfully breastfeed.

Older Adults
Engage in regular physical activity to reduce functional declines associated with aging.

Source: USDA Dietary Guidelines for Americans 2005, Physical Activity, viii.

Engaging in regular physical activity will promote your health, psychological well-being and a healthy body weight. Use the following recommendations for achieving regular physical activity.

- To reduce the risk of chronic disease in adulthood, engage in at least 30 minutes of moderate-intensity physical activity. Physical activity should be above usual activity at work or home on most days of the week.

- Greater health benefits can be achieved by most people by engaging in more vigorous physical activity over a longer duration.

- To help manage body weight and to prevent gradual unhealthy weight gain in adulthood, engage in approximately 60 minutes of moderate to vigorous intensity activity on most days of the week, while not exceeding caloric intake requirements.

- To sustain weight loss in adulthood, participate in at least 60 to 90 minutes of daily moderate-intensity physical activity while not exceeding caloric intake requirements.

- Achieve physical fitness by including cardiovascular conditioning, stretching exercises for flexibility and resistance exercises or calisthenics for muscle strength and endurance.

Calories Expended in Common Physical Activities

This table shows the average amount of calories expended during common physical activities. Examples are average amounts of calories a 154•pound individual will expend by engaging in each activity for 1 hour. The expenditure value encompasses both resting metabolic rate calories and activity expenditure. Some of the activities can constitute either moderate- or vigorous-intensity physical activity depending on the rate at which they are carried out (for example, walking or biking).

Moderate Physical Activity	Approximate Calories Expended Per Hour
Hiking	370
Light gardening/yard work	330
Dancing	330
Golf (walking while carrying clubs)	330
Bicycling (<10 mph)	290
Walking (3.5 mph)	280
Weight lifting (general light workout)	220
Stretching	180

Vigorous Physical Activity	
Running/jogging (5 mph)	590
Bicycling (>10 mph)	590
Swimming (slow freestyle laps)	510
Aerobics	480
Walking (4.5 mph)	460
Heavy yard work (chopping wood)	440
Weight lifting (vigorous effort)	440
Basketball (vigorous)	440

Source: *USDA Dietary Guidelines for Americans 2005, Table 4.*

Household Hints

Tips to remedy this or that in the household

Clean-up Tips 2-3

Keeping Furniture Clean 4-5

Laundry Care 6

Removing Clothing Stains 7

Removing Floor Stains 8

Basic Fabric Care 9

Food Safety 10

Kitchen Safety 11

Perfect Party Checklist 12

Menu Planning 13

Table Settings 14

Buffet Arrangement 15

Staying Organized 16

Clean-up Tips

Appliances: To shine chrome, use vinegar or window cleaner. If the numbers on your oven dial are worn, take a yellow crayon and rub it all over the number on the dial. Gently wipe off the excess crayon and paint with clear nail polish. To clean splattered food from the interior of your microwave, bring one cup of water to a boil until steam forms on the inside walls of microwave. Remove water and wipe with a damp cloth. You may have to repeat the process to get a really big job done.

To rid yellowing from white appliances try this: Mix together: ½ cup bleach, ¼ cup baking soda and 4 cups warm water. Apply with a sponge and let set for 10 minutes. Rinse and dry thoroughly. Instead of using commercial waxes, shine with rubbing alcohol. For quick clean-ups, rub with equal parts of water and household ammonia. Or, try club soda. It cleans and polishes at the same time.

Blender: Fill part way with hot water and add a drop of detergent. Cover and turn it on for a few seconds. Rinse and drain dry.

Burnt and scorched pans: Sprinkle burnt pans liberally with baking soda, adding just enough water to moisten. Let stand for several hours. You can generally lift the burned portions right out of the pan.

Stubborn stains on non-stick cookware can be removed by boiling 2 tablespoons of baking soda, ½ cup vinegar and 1 cup water for 10 minutes. Re-season pan with salad oil.

Cast-iron skillets: Clean the outside of the pan with commercial oven cleaner. Let set for 2 hours and the accumulated black stains can be removed with vinegar and water.

Dishwasher: Run a cup of white vinegar through the entire cycle in an empty dishwasher to remove all soap film.

Clogged drains: When a drain is clogged with grease, pour a cup of salt and a cup of baking soda into the drain followed by a kettle of boiling water. The grease will usually dissolve immediately and open the drain.

Coffee grounds are a no-no. They do a nice job of clogging, especially if they get mixed with grease.

Dusting: Spray furniture polish on the bristles of your broom and the dust and dirt will be easier to collect when you sweep.

Dish Drainer: Remove hard water stains from your dish drainer by tilting the low end of the board slightly and pouring one cup of white vinegar over the board. Let it set overnight and rub off with a sponge in the morning.

Glassware: Never put a delicate glass in hot water bottom side first; it will crack from sudden expansion. The most delicate glassware will be safe if it is slipped in edgewise.

Vinegar is a must when washing crystal. Rinse in 1 part vinegar to 3 parts warm water. Air dry.

When one glass is tucked inside another, do not force them apart. Fill the top glass with cold water and dip the lower one in hot water. They will come apart without breaking.

Grater: For a fast and simple clean-up, rub salad oil on the grater before using.

Use a toothbrush to brush lemon rind, cheese, onion or whatever out of the grater before washing.

Thermos bottle: Fill the bottle with warm water, add 1 teaspoon of baking soda and allow to soak.

Oven: Following a spill, sprinkle with salt immediately. When oven is cool, brush off burnt food and wipe with a damp sponge.

Sprinkle bottom of oven with automatic dishwasher soap and cover with wet paper towels. Let stand for a few hours.

A quick way to clean oven parts is to place a bath towel in the bathtub and pile all removable parts from the oven onto it. Draw enough hot water to just cover the parts and sprinkle a cup of dishwasher soap over it. While you are cleaning the inside of the oven, the rest will be cleaning itself.

An inexpensive oven cleaner: Set oven on warm for about 20 minutes, then turn off. Place a small dish of full strength ammonia on the top shelf. Put a large pan of boiling water on the bottom shelf and let it set overnight. In the morning, open oven and let it air a while before washing off with soap and water. Even the hard baked-on grease will wash off easily.

Plastic cups, dishes and containers: Coffee or tea stains can be scoured with baking soda.

Or, fill the stained cup with hot water and drop in a few denture cleanser tablets. Let soak for 1 hour.

To rid foul odors from plastic containers, place crumpled-up newspaper (black and white only) into the container. Cover tightly and leave overnight.

Refrigerator: To help eliminate odors fill a small bowl with charcoal (the kind used for potted plants) and place it on a shelf in the refrigerator. It absorbs odors rapidly.

An open box of baking soda will absorb food odors for at least a month or two.

A little vanilla poured on a piece of cotton and placed in the refrigerator will eliminate odors.

To prevent mildew from forming, wipe with vinegar. The acid effectively kills the mildew fungus. Use a glycerin soaked cloth to wipe sides and shelves. Future spills wipe up easily.

After the freezer has been defrosted, coat the inside coils with glycerin. The next time you defrost, the ice will loosen quickly and drop off in sheets.

Wash inside and out with a mixture of 3 tablespoons of baking soda in a quart of warm water.

Sinks: For a sparkling white sink, place paper towels across the bottom of your sink and saturate with household bleach. Let set for ½ hour or so.

Rub stainless steel sinks with lighter fluid if rust marks appear. After the rust disappears wipe with your regular kitchen cleanser.

Use a cloth dampened with rubbing alcohol to remove water spots from stainless steel.

Spots on stainless steel can also be removed with white vinegar. Club soda will shine up stainless steel sinks in a jiffy.

Teakettle: To remove lime deposits, fill with equal parts of vinegar and water. Bring to a boil and allow to stand overnight.

Keeping Furniture Clean

To remove polish build-up: Mix ½ cup vinegar and ½ cup water. Rub with a soft cloth that has been moistened with solution, but wrung out. Dry immediately with another soft cloth.

Polishing carved furniture: Dip an old soft toothbrush into furniture polish and brush lightly.

Cigarette burns: For small minor burns, try rubbing mayonnaise into the burn. Let set for a while before wiping off with a soft cloth.

Burns can be repaired with a wax stick (available in all colors at paint and hardware stores). Gently scrape away the charred finish. Heat a knife blade and melt the shellac stick against the heated blade. Smooth over damaged area with your finger. But always consider the value of the furniture. It might be better to have a professional make the repair.

Or, make a paste of rottenstone (available at hardware stores) and salad oil. Rub into the burned spot only, following the grain of wood. Wipe clean with a cloth that has been dampened in oil. Wipe dry and apply your favorite furniture polish.

Removing paper that is stuck to a wood surface: Do not scrape with a knife. Pour any salad oil, a few drops at a time, on the paper. Let set for a while and rub with a soft cloth. Repeat the procedure until the paper is completely gone.

Old decals can be removed easily by painting them with several coats of white vinegar. Give the vinegar time to soak in, then gently scrape off.

Scratches: Make sure you always rub with the grain of the wood when repairing a scratch.

Walnut: Remove the meat from a fresh, unsalted walnut or pecan nut. Break it in half and rub the scratch with the broken side of the nut.

Mahogany: You can either rub the scratch with a dark brown crayon or buff with brown paste wax.

Red Mahogany: Apply ordinary iodine with a number 0 artist's brush.

Maple: Combine equal amounts of iodine and denatured alcohol. Apply with a Q-tip, then dry, wax and buff.

Ebony: Use black shoe polish, black eyebrow pencil or black crayon.

Teakwood: Rub very gently with 0000 steel wool. Rub in equal amounts of linseed oil and turpentine.

Light-finished furniture: Scratches can be hidden by using tan shoe polish. However, only on shiny finishes.

For all minor scratches: Cover each scratch with a generous amount of white petroleum jelly. Allow it to remain on for 24 hours. Rub into wood. Remove excess and polish as usual.

For larger scratches: Fill by rubbing with a wax stick (available in all colors at your hardware or paint store) or a crayon that matches the finish of the wood.

Three solutions to remove white water rings and spots: Dampen a soft cloth with water and put a dab of toothpaste on it. For stubborn stains, add baking soda to the toothpaste.

Make a paste of butter or mayonnaise and cigarette ashes. Apply to spot and buff away.

Apply a paste of salad oil and salt. Let stand briefly. Wipe and polish.

Marble table-top stains: Sprinkle salt on a fresh-cut lemon. Rub very lightly over stain. Do not rub hard or you will ruin the polished surface. Wash off with soap and water.

Scour with a water and baking soda paste. Let stand for a few minutes before rinsing with warm water.

Removing candle wax from wooden finishes: Soften the wax with a hair dryer. Remove wax with paper toweling and wash down with a solution of vinegar and water.

Plastic table tops: You will find that a coat of Turtle Wax is a quick pick-up for dulled plastic table tops and counters.

Or, rub in toothpaste and buff.

Glass table tops: Rub in a little lemon juice. Dry with paper towels and shine with newspaper for a sparkling table.

Toothpaste will remove small scratches from glass.

Chrome cleaning: For sparkling clean chrome without streaks, use a cloth dampened in ammonia.

Removing glue: Cement glue can be removed by rubbing with cold cream, peanut butter or salad oil.

Wicker: Wicker needs moisture, so use a humidifier in the winter. To prevent drying out, apply lemon oil occasionally.

Never let wicker freeze. This will cause cracking and splitting.

Wash with a solution of warm salt water to keep from turning yellow.

Metal furniture: To remove rust, a good scrubbing with turpentine should accomplish this job.

Vinyl upholstery: Never oil vinyl as this will make it hard. It is almost impossible to soften again. For proper cleaning, sprinkle baking soda or vinegar on a rough, damp cloth, then wash with a mild dishwashing soap.

Soiled upholstery: Rub soiled cotton upholstery fabric with an artgum eraser or squares (purchased at stationery store).

Leather upholstery: Prevent leather from cracking by polishing regularly with a cream made of 1 part vinegar and 2 parts linseed oil. Clean with a damp cloth and saddle soap.

Grease stains: Absorb grease on furniture by pouring salt on the spill immediately.

Laundry Care

Spot removal: Two parts water and one part rubbing alcohol are the basic ingredients in any commercial spot remover.

Clean machine: Fill your washer with warm water and add a gallon of distilled vinegar. Run the machine through the entire cycle to unclog and clean soap scum from hoses.

Too sudsy: When your washer overflows with too many suds, sprinkle salt in the water – the suds will disappear.

Hand-washed sweaters: Add a capful of hair cream rinse to the final rinse water when washing sweaters.

Whiter fabric: Linen or cotton can be whitened by boiling in a mixture or 1 part cream of tartar and 3 parts water.

Whitest socks: Boil socks in water to which a lemon slice has been added.

Freshen feather pillows: Put feather pillows in the dryer and tumble, then air outside.

Lintless corduroy: While corduroy is still damp, brush with clothes brush to remove all lint.

Ironing tip: When pressing pants, iron the top part on the wrong side. Iron the legs on the right side. This gives the pockets and waistband a smooth look.

Creaseless garments: Take an empty cardboard paper towel roll and cut through it lengthwise. Slip it over a wire hanger to prevent a crease from forming in the garment to be hung on the hanger.

Remove creases from hems: Sponge material with a white vinegar solution and press flat to remove creases in hems.

Bedroom ironing: A good place to iron is in the bedroom. Closets are nearby to hang clothes up immediately, and the bed makes a good surface on which to fold clothes and separate items into piles.

Ironing board cover: When washing your ironing board cover, attach it to the board while it is still damp. When it dries, the surface will be completely smooth. Starch your ironing board cover. This helps the cover stay clean longer.

Lint remover: Add a yard of nylon netting to your dryer with the wet clothes – it will catch most of the lint.

Washer advice: Button all buttons on clothing and turn inside out before putting into the washer. Fewer buttons will fall off and garments will fade less if turned inside out.

Soiled collars: Use a small paintbrush and brush hair shampoo into soiled shirt collars before laundering. Shampoo is made to dissolve body oils.

Faster ironing: Place a strip of heavy-duty aluminum foil over the entire length of the ironing board and cover with pad. As you iron, heat will reflect through the underside of the garment.

Ironing embroidery: Lay the embroidery piece upside-down on a Turkish towel before ironing. All the little spaces between the embroidery will be smooth when you are finished.

Removing Clothing Stains

Alcoholic beverages: Pre-soak or sponge fresh stains immediately with cold water, then with cold water and glycerin. Rinse with vinegar for a few seconds if stain remains. These stains may turn brown with age. If wine stain remains, rub with concentrated detergent; wait 15 minutes; rinse. Repeat if necessary. Wash with detergent in hottest water safe for fabric.

Baby Food: Use liquid laundry detergent and brush into stain with an old toothbrush then wash.

Blood: Pre-soak in cold or warm water at least 30 minutes. If stain remains, soak in lukewarm ammonia water (3 tablespoons per gallon water). Rinse. If stain remains, work in detergent, and wash, using bleach safe for fabric.

Candle wax: Use a dull knife to scrape off as much as possible. Place fabric between 2 blotters or facial tissues and press with warm iron. Remove color stain with non-flammable dry cleaning solvent. Wash with detergent in the hottest water safe for fabric.

Chewing gum: Rub area with ice, then scrape off with a dull blade. Sponge with dry cleaning solvent; allow to air dry. Wash in detergent and hottest water safe for fabric.

Cosmetics: Loosen stain with a non-flammable dry cleaning solvent. Rub detergent in until stain outline is gone. Wash in hottest water and detergent safe for fabric.

Deodorants: Sponge area with white vinegar. If stain remains, soak with denatured alcohol. Wash with detergent in hottest water safe for fabric.

Dye: If dye transfers from a non-colorfast item during washing, immediately bleach discolored items. Repeat as necessary BEFORE drying. On whites use color remover. *CAUTION:* Do not use color remover in washer, or around washer and dryer as it may damage the finish.

Fruit and fruit juices: Sponge with cold water. Pre-soak in cold or warm water for at least 30 minutes. Wash with detergent and bleach safe for fabric.

Grass: Pre-soak in cold water for at least 30 minutes. Rinse. Pre-treat with detergent, hot water, and bleach safe for fabric. On acetate and colored fabrics, use 1 part of alcohol to 2 parts water.

Grease, oil, tar or butter: *Method 1:* Use powder or chalk absorbents to remove as much grease as possible. Pre-treat with detergent or non-flammable dry cleaning solvent, or liquid shampoo. Wash in hottest water safe for fabric, using plenty of detergent.

Method 2: Rub spot with lard and sponge with a non-flammable dry cleaning solvent. Wash in hottest water and detergent safe for fabric.

Perspiration: Sponge fresh stain with ammonia; old stain with vinegar. Pre-soak in cold or warm water. Rinse. Wash in hottest water safe for fabric. If fabric is yellowed, use bleach. If stain still remains, dampen and sprinkle with meat tenderizer, or pepsin. Let stand 1 hour. Brush off and wash. For persistent odor, sponge with colorless mouthwash.

Household Hints – 7

Removing Floor Stains

Candle drippings: For spilled wax on carpet, use a brown paper bag as a blotter and run a hot iron over it, which will absorb the wax.

Dog stains: Blot up excess moisture with paper towel. Pour club soda on the spot and continue blotting. Lay a towel over the spot and set a heavy object on top in order to absorb all the moisture.

Rug care: When washing and drying foam-backed throw rugs, never wash in hot water, and use the "air only" dryer setting to dry. Heat will ruin foam.

Cleaning rugs: If the rug is only slightly dirty, you can clean it with cornmeal. Use a stiff brush to work the cornmeal into the pile of the rug. Take it all out with the vacuum.

Spills on the rug: When spills happen, go to the bathroom and grab a can of shaving cream. Squirt it on the spot then rinse off with water.

Ballpoint ink marks: Saturate the spots with hairspray. Allow to dry. Brush lightly with a solution of water and vinegar.

Glue: Glue can be loosened by saturating the spot with a cloth soaked in vinegar.

Repairing braided rugs: Braided rugs often rip apart. Instead of sewing them, use clear fabric glue to repair. It's that fast and easy.

Repairing a burn: Remove some fuzz from the carpet, either by shaving or pulling out with a tweezer. Roll into the shape of the burn. Apply a good cement glue to the backing of the rug and press the fuzz down into the burned spot. Cover with a piece of cleansing tissue and place a heavy book on top. This will cause the glue to dry very slowly and will get the best results.

Spot remover for outdoor carpeting: Spray spots liberally with a pre-wash commercial spray. Let it set several minutes, then hose down and watch the spots disappear.

Blood on the rug: When you get blood on your rug, rub off as much as you can at first, then take a cloth soaked in cold water and wet the spot, wiping it up as you go. If a little bit remains, pour some ammonia onto the cool, wet cloth and lightly wipe that over the spot, too. Rinse it right away with cold water.

Crayon Marks: Use silver polish to remove from vinyl tile or linoleum.

Spilled nail polish: Allow to almost dry, then peel off of waxed floors or tile.

Tar spots: Use paste wax to remove tar from floors. Works on shoes, too.

Dusting floors: Stretch a nylon stocking over the dust mop. After using, discard the stocking and you will have a clean mop.

Varnished floors: Use cold tea to clean woodwork and varnished floors.

Spilled grease: Rub floor with ice cubes to solidify grease. Scrape up excess and wash with soapy water.

Quick shine: Put a piece of waxed paper under your dust mop. Dirt will stick to the mop and the wax will shine your floors.

Unmarred floors: Put thick old socks over the legs of heavy furniture when moving across floors.

Wood floor care: Never use water or water-based cleaners on wood floors. Over a period of time, warping and swelling will develop.

Heel marks: Just take a pencil eraser and wipe them off.

Floor polisher: When cleaning the felt pads of your floor polisher, place the pads between layers of newspaper and press with an iron to absorb built-up wax.

Garage floors: In an area where a large amount of oil has spilled, lay several thicknesses of newspaper. Saturate the paper with water; press flat against the floor. When dry, remove the newspaper and the spots will have disappeared.

Basement floors: Sprinkle sand on oily spots, let it absorb the oil, and sweep up.

Basic Fabric Care

Keep your clothing and fabrics looking and feeling great by following a few basic washing, drying and ironing rules. Be sure to follow any specific instructions on the care label of clothing pieces. Take tailored clothes and special items to a dry cleaner.

Fabric	Washing	Drying & Ironing
Acetates	Machine or hand wash at a low temperature. Do not wring or fast spin in machine.	Do not tumble dry. Allow acetate items to dry naturally and iron while still damp.
Acrylic	Usually machine washable – check label. Wash at low temperature.	Pull into shape after washing and remove excess water. Dry flat or line dry.
Brocade	Hand wash at cool temperature or dry clean. Do not wring.	Iron on the wrong side over a towel.
Cashmere	Hand wash in cool water in well-dissolved soap. Rinse well. Do not wring.	Dry and gently pull into shape. Iron inside out while damp with a cool iron.
Corduroy	Always wash inside out. Hand or machine wash – check label.	Iron inside out while evenly damp. Smooth fabric with a soft cloth.
Cotton	Machine wash at high temperature, separating whites from colors.	Tumble or line dry. Iron before items are completely dry.
Denim	Wash separately until there is no color run. Wash items inside out.	Tumble or line dry. Iron while very damp with a hot iron.
Leather & Suede	Protect items with leather spray after hand washing.	Rub suede onto another piece of suede or use a suede brush.
Linen	Machine wash according to label.	Iron while damp. Starch to prevent creases.
Silk	Hand wash in warm water. Some items may be machine washed on delicate cycle.	Line dry naturally and iron while damp. Use a pressing cloth to protect fabric.
Wool	Hand wash unless machine is acceptable – check label.	Dry flat, line dry or use a sweater rack. Do not tumble dry.

Food Safety

Keep your family and yourself healthy by ensuring the foods you consume have been purchased, stored and prepared safely. A general understanding of how germs and bacteria grow will help protect you and your family from the risk of food poisoning.

When Shopping

- Carefully check over fresh fruits and vegetables for bruising, rotting or discoloration.
- Try to keep chilled and frozen foods as cold as possible between buying these items and storage at home. Once home, transfer these foods to the refrigerator or freezer immediately.
- Read all package labels carefully, noting the expiration date and any ingredients that may affect a family member by causing an allergic reaction.

When Storing

- Make sure your refrigerator is running correctly and kept cold enough, as harmful bacteria will flourish in warmer temperatures. Keep the coldest part of the refrigerator around 0 to 5°C/32 to 41°F.
- Store the most perishable foods in the coldest part of the refrigerator.
- Place foods that should be kept cooler, such as milk, fruit juices, cheeses, butter and eggs, in the refrigerator's special compartments.
- Wrap and cover all raw and uncooked foods to prevent them from touching other foods.
- Discard foods that have been kept longer than the "use by" or "best before" date.

When Preparing

- Keep your hands and all equipment extremely clean.
- Never use a knife that has been used to cut raw meat or fish for anything else before washing it thoroughly.
- Use separate cutting boards for raw foods, vegetables and cooked meats.
- Carefully wash and disinfect cutting boards, counter surfaces and kitchen towels after all uses.
- High temperatures will kill most bacteria. Be sure to cook foods throughout, especially raw meats and fish. A good rule of thumb is to cook meats so the center reaches 70°C/158°F for at least 2 minutes.
- Cooking raw eggs will destroy bacteria. Avoid recipes calling for uncooked eggs.
- It is best to thaw frozen foods in the refrigerator or microwave. If frozen meats or fish are not completely thawed, the center may not cook properly.
- Never reheat food or meals more than once.

Kitchen Safety

Kitchen Fires

Always keep a domestic fire extinguisher in the kitchen. However, be careful not to position the extinguisher above the stove, as a stovetop or oven fire would make the extinguisher inaccessible. Be sure to train your entire family on how to use the fire extinguisher. A compact fire blanket kept close will help suffocate flames from deep-fat fryers, which are a major cause of household fires. NEVER throw water on grease fires!

Child Safety

Use cupboard lock handles so children and infants cannot get into harmful kitchen chemicals or other products. Buy detergents and cleaning chemicals that have child-proof lids or store these products in high cupboards or on high shelves that are out of reach. Never leave knives or scissors on the counter. Try to keep them out of the way by placing them in a lockable drawer, on a magnetic rack or in a wooden knife block.

Hygiene

Always wash hands in warm soapy water before touching food, after touching raw foods and before touching ready-to-eat foods. If cuts or scrapes occur while cooking food, be sure to wash and cover the area immediately. Wipe hands on a separate kitchen towel, reserving the dish towel for dishes only. Bleach, disinfect or replace kitchen towels, cloths and sponges often, especially after working with raw foods. Return perishable foods, such as butter or milk, to the refrigerator as soon as possible after use.

Hot Pans

On the stovetop, make sure pan handles are pointing inwards so they won't be knocked off or catch on loose clothing. When using a frying pan, place a splatter guard over the pan so you or others will not be splattered by hot oil or grease.

Perfect Party Checklist

- [ ] Create the party guest list.
- [ ] If applicable, pick a party theme. Party themes can be helpful during the planning process, as they give the party a defined purpose and focus.
- [ ] As party ideas come to you, jot them down. Don't rely on your memory for thoughts and inspiration.
- [ ] Create/buy invitations and send. If you have a theme, use the invitations to incorporate the theme and as a way to get party guests excited for the event!
- [ ] Gather materials needed for serving food, party games, decorations, music and/or party favors.
- [ ] Create the party menu, including snacks, main meal, beverages and/or dessert.
- [ ] Buy all necessary food and ingredients. If possible, prepare as much food the day before or morning of the party. If necessary, chill the beverages.
- [ ] Set the mood with decorations, lighting and music.
- [ ] Don't forget to wear something that is comfortable but, as the party host, makes you feel special!
- [ ] Set out party snacks, beverages, decorations and favors.
- [ ] Relax and welcome your guests!

Menu Planning

When Selecting Recipes for a Party

- Plan the main course first, unless a meal will not be served. After choosing the main course, pick appetizers, sides and desserts to complement it.
- Keep the courses simple and try to choose items that can be either entirely or partly prepared ahead of time.
- Try to create a balance of color, texture and flavor throughout the courses. Avoid choosing recipes that are too similar, for example, all egg- or cheese-based.
- Balance a rich or spicy dish with a plain, light and/or refreshing appetizer or dessert.
- Be aware of any special dietary or allergic requirements your guests may have.
- Unless you have extra help, try to limit the amount of courses to three.

Estimating Quantities

Food	10 Portions	20 Portions	40 Portions
Soup	1/2 gallon	1 gallon	2 gallons
Cold, sliced meats	2 lbs.	3 lbs. 14 oz.	7 lbs. 11 oz.
Boneless meat for casseroles	2 lbs. 3 oz.	5 lbs.	10 lbs.
Roast meat on the bone	3 lbs. 14 oz.	6 lbs. 10 oz.	14 lbs. 5 oz.
Cheese	12 oz.	2 lbs.	2 lbs. 12 oz.
Crackers for cheese	1 lb. 1 oz.	1 lb. 10 oz.	2 lbs. 3 oz.
Filleted fish	2 lbs. 12 oz.	5 lbs.	10 lbs.
Whole chicken or turkey	7 lbs. 11 oz.	15 lbs. 7 oz.	2 – 7 lbs. 11 oz.
Rice or pasta (uncooked weight)	1 lb. 1 oz.	1 lb. 9 oz.	2 lbs. 12 oz.
Fresh fruits or fruit salad	3 lbs. 5 oz.	6 lbs. 1 oz.	12 lbs. 2 oz.
Ice cream	1/2 gallon	3/4 gallon	1 1/4 gallons

Table Settings

For a Full-Course Meal

For a Casual Meal

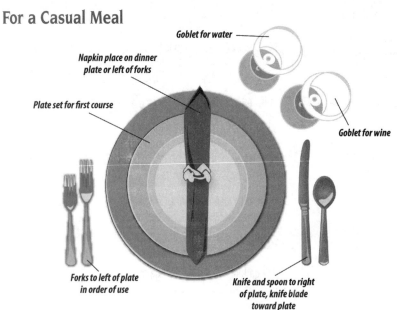

Buffet Arrangement

Arranging the Buffet Table

- Decide which direction guests will walk around the table.
- Start with empty plates, then side dishes, followed by the main dish and finally the vegetables and salads. Place serving utensils beside each dish.
- Set breads, relishes, cutlery and napkins at the end of the table. If there is room, set decorations in the center of the table.
- Leave room behind the buffet table so you have easy access for replacing dishes.
- Leave spaces between dishes on the buffet table so guests can set down glasses or plates when serving themselves.
- To keep cold side dishes or salads chilled, set the serving bowl or dish inside a separate dish that is full of ice.
- Place drinks, glasses, cups and ice on a separate table to avoid congestion in one area.

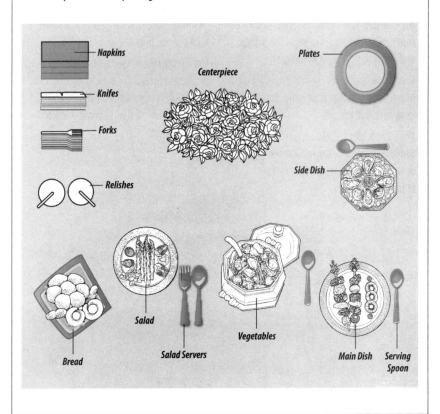

Household Hints – 15

Staying Organized

Use the following tips to keep your home organized.

- Use drawer dividers to give smaller items a well-defined spot. Within the drawers, store very small items in jewelry boxes, ice cube trays, desk trays, etc.
- Label storage containers or boxes with pictures or words so everyone will know the contents within. Color-coding works well, too. Color-code items for certain areas. For example, yellow-tagged items go in the upstairs bathroom. Or, use a separate color for each family member.
- Store items close to where they are used. For example, store jumper cables in the car trunk, pens and paper close to the phone and fast-food coupons in the car.
- Keep separate folders holding data for the home, for each car, for pets and for tax and insurance documents.
- Use a file folder to hold receipts for valuable items. File any guarantees or warranties together with the appropriate receipt.
- Print hard copies of important documents on your computer and file the documents in a safe place. This will allow you to retrieve the documents in case the computer breaks down or is stolen.
- If you keep magazines or pamphlets that do not show their title or issue on the spine, group the items by title and sort in a magazine file. Place a label on the file showing the contents within.
- Combine all cleaning fluids, detergents and rags needed to clean a particular area or room. Place them together in a sturdy container or bucket.
- Use lists to remember items needed, important errands or appointments. If possible, carry the list with you and check the items off as they are gathered or completed.

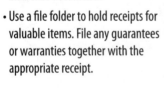

INDEX

Appetizers, Beverages & Dips

Bailey's Irish Cream 9
Banana Berry Shake 8
Bean Dip 2
Beer Dip 1
Brandy Slush 9
Braunschweiger Party Dip 1
Cappuccino Mix 7
Cheesy Crab Roll Ups 7
Cherry Bounce (Liquor) 9
Chicken Jalapeno Dip 2
Chipped Beef Dip 1
Florida Caviar 4
Frosty Orange Juice 8
Olive Cheese Balls 5
Oriental Chicken Dip 2
Praline Coffee 8
Salmon Ball 6
Salmon Mousse 7
Salsa Fresca (Fresh Salsa) 3
Shrimp Ball 6
Spiced Tea 8
Taco Dip 3
Texas Caviar 4
Three In One Cheese Ball 5

Soups & Salads

1000 Island Dressing 29
Bean Soup 18
Beef Barley Soup 11
Beef Tortellini Soup 12
Blt Pasta Salad 21
Buttermilk Fruit Salad 30
Calico Bean Soup 19
California Medly 18
Chicken Noodle Soup 12
Chicken Pasta Salad 20
Chicken Taco Salad 23
Chinese Salad 22
Clam Chowder 14
Classic Waldorf Salad 27
Corn & Sausage Chowder 13
Crab Pasta Salad 22
Crab Salad 24
Cream Of Asparagus Soup 13
Cream Of Broccoli Soup 16
Grilled Chicken Salad 25
Jicama Salad 26
Kitchen Sink Salad 29
Nutty Chicken Salad 26
Potato Salad 30
Potato Soup 15
Raw Veggie Salad 25
Seafood Noodle Salad 20
Sesame Chicken Salad 24
Seven Layer Salad 26
Simple Lemon Dressing 29
Spaghetti Soup 12
Split Pea Soup 15
Strawberry Spinach Salad 28
Stuffed Green Pepper Soup ... 11
Taco Salad 23
Taco Soup 17
Tomato Basil Soup 16
Tortellini Caesar Salad 21
Tuna Salad 27
Variation Waldorf Salad 28
Vegetable Cheese Soup 17
White Chili 19
Wisconsin Beer Cheese Soup 14

Breads & Rolls

Beer Bread (The Easiest Bread Recipe Ever) 31
Buttermilk Bread (Bread Maker Recipe) 31
Chocolate Zucchini Bread 34
Ever Ready Bran Muffins (Our Family's Traditional Easter Breakfast) 35
Flour Tortillas 32
Gingerbread Pancakes 37
Lemon Poppyseed Bread 34
Lemony Zucchini Bread 33
Oatmeal Apple Raisin Muffins 36
Oatmeal Bread (Bread Maker Recipe) 31
Oatmeal Pancakes 36
Peanut Butter Bread 32
Pecan Pumpkin Bread 33
Pizza Dough 32
Zucchini Bread / Muffins 35

Vegetables & Side Dishes

Calico Beans 42
Creamed Corn Casserole 39
German Spaetzle 39
Hash Brown Casserole 41
Mom's Home Made Egg Noodles 39
Oven Baked Potato Wedges .. 40
Scalloped Potatoes 40
Sliced Baked Potatoes 41
Vegetable Pizza 42

Main Dishes & Meats

Beef Stroganoff 46
Beef Tips 46
Chicken Casserole 53
Chicken Divan 51
Chicken Enchiladas 50
Chicken Spaghetti 52
Chicken Stir Fry 48
Chop Suey 47
Crab Quesadillas 54
Deep Dish Pizza 45
Grilled Tilapia 53
Jerry Burger 47
Lasagna 44
Meatloaf 44
Mexican Casserole 51
Mexican Lasagna 49
Peas 'N' Rice Hot Dish 43
Pizza Hot Dish 45
Quick And Easy Chicken Pot Pie 52
Spagetti And Meatballs 43
Spicy Broccoli Beef Stir Fry 48
Spicy Tortilla Bake 49
Three Cheese Enchiladas 50

Desserts

Angel Torte 66
Apple Cake 76
Apple Slices 67
Better Than Sex Cake 72
Blueberry Torte 64
Butterfinger Pie 55
Butterscotch Pie 56
Carrot Cake 75
Cheese Danish 67
Cherry Surprise 64
Chocolate Chip Cheesecake Bars 63
Chocolate Crumb Crust 61

Chocolate Lovers
  Cheesecake 62
Chocolate Zucchini Cake 74
Cocoa Cola Cake 75
Coconut Cream Dessert 65
Coconut Cream Pie 58
Coconut Fudge Pie 58
Creamy Frozen Lime Pie 60
Dirt Cake 73
Dump Cake 72
French Lemon Bars 68
Fresh Raspberry Pie 59
Fruit Coffee Cake 71
Fruit Pizza 71
Graham Cracker Crust 61
Lemon Berry Trifle 76
Peanut Butter Pie 60
Pecan Pie 57
Pineapple Upside Down
  Cake (The Way Mom Made
  It In The 50'S) 73
Polish Drumsticks 65
Pumpkin Bars 69
Pumpkin Cheese Pie 57
Pumpkin Cheesecake Bars 63
Pumpkin Crunch 68
Quick And Easy Cherry
  Cheesecake 62
Rhubarb Cake 70
Rhubarb Cobbler 70
Rhubarb Custard Pie 55
Rhubarb Dream Bars 69
Sour Cream Cheesecake 61
Strawberry Pie 59
Streusel Topped Pumpkin Pie .. 56
Toffee Cheesecake 62
Waverly Tort 66
Whipped Strawberry Cream
  Pie 60
Zucchini Cake 74

Cookies & Candies

Amish Sugar Cookies 79
Big Mac Cookies 80
Black Forest Brownie Bars 84
Boat Bars 83
Buffalo Chips 78
Buttery Oatmeal Turtle Bars 82
Caramel Nut Brownies 84
Caramels 86
Chocolate Billionares 87
Chocolate Mint Sticks 85
Coconut Oatmeal Cookies 78
Cream Cheese After Dinner
  Mints 88
English Toffee (Heath Bars) 87
Fruit Bars 82
Fudge (As Good As Fanny
  Farmer) 86
Gingersnaps 79
Kisses In The Dark 79
Kit Kat Bars 83
Molasses Cookies 80
Mom's Chocolate Chip
  Cookies 77
Peanut Butter Fudge 86
Sandies 77
Seven Layer Bars 81
Stained Glass (Hard Candy) ... 88
Starlight Mint Surprise
  Cookies 81
Sugar 'N Spice Nuts 85
Toffee 87

Miscellaneous

Breakfast Casserole 89
Breakfast Pizza 89
Cherry Fruit Cake 91

Easy Microwave Baked
   Apples 90
Fruit And Nut Granola 91
Funnel Cake 92
Orange Dreamsicle Dessert ... 93
Oven Omelet 89
Pumpkin Pudding 92
Scalloped Apples 90
Sopapillas 92
Stuffed French Toast 90

How to Order

Order additional copies of this cookbook as an ideal gift for family and friends.

Send check or money order along with order form below to:

The Nuts & Bolts of Soup to Nuts Cooking
Soup to Nuts
PO Box 35 • Crivitz, WI 54114
Phone: 715-854-2000
Email: crivitz.souptonuts@gmail.com
Website: www.souptonutscrivitz.com

✂ -

Please send me _____ copies of your cookbook at $11.95 each, plus $2.00 shipping and handling per book ordered.
Mail books to:

Name _____

Address _____

City _____

State _____ Zip _____

✂ -

Please send me _____ copies of your cookbook at $11.95 each, plus $2.00 shipping and handling per book ordered.
Mail books to:

Name _____

Address _____

City _____

State _____ Zip _____

Love Cookbooks?
So Do We!

Cookbooks are a wonderful way to share one of life's true pleasures – delicious food. For many families, favorite recipes are a cherished heirloom, and creating a cookbook is a great way to preserve these treasures for future generations. For fundraisers, cookbooks are an easy sell; buyers are lured with the promise of their neighbor's and friend's trusted recipes!

For more than 35 years, G&R Publishing has enjoyed helping families, churches, schools, groups and fundraisers create custom cookbooks.

We'd love to help you create a custom cookbook too. Simply send your recipes to G&R or enter your recipes online at www.gandrpublishing.com. It's that easy! For more information, please visit our website or call 800-383-1679 for a free cookbook guide.

Thank you for purchasing this book. We hope you'll enjoy using it!

507 Industrial Street
Waverly, IA 50677
800-383-1679
books@gandrpublishing.com
www.gandrpublishing.com